Court And Kitchen

Of

Elizabeth

Commonly called

Joan Cromwell,

The

Wife of the late Usurper,

Truly

Described and Represented,

And now

Made Public for general

Satisfaction.

London, Printed by Tho(mas) Milbourn, for Randal Taylor
in St. Martins Le Grand, 1664.

Glossary and notes by Mary Liquorice, F.L.A.
Preface by Douglas Clinton, B.A., B.Phil.

Cambridgeshire Libraries gratefully acknowledges the help
received from:—
Cambridge Folk Museum for loan of cooking utensils used on
front cover photograph;
Cromwell Museum for permission to reproduce the original
book and for loan of photographs and engravings;
Miss L. E. Braddick, John Mills and John Dexter for help with
translations.
Mrs. Ann Short for typing.

Reprinted with amendments, notes and glossary by
Cambridgeshire Libraries, Publications Committee, c/o
Central Library, Broadway, Peterborough, 1983.

Designed & Printed by Heffers Printers Limited, Cambridge.
Cover Photographs by Reeve Photography, Cambridge: Art
Directed by Heffers.

PREFACE

"*T*he Court and Kitchin of Elizabeth Cromwell" is a purely satirical work but a pamphlet with a difference – both a slanderous attack on the Lord Protector and Lady Protectress and a somewhat disordered cookbook. The flood of invective hurled by the author against Oliver Cromwell and his family served two purposes: as retribution for the libels against the first two Stuarts and as a declaration of loyalty to the new regime. Further impetus was given by the fact that the Cromwell family escaped ill-treatment at the Restoration: Elizabeth Cromwell, for example, was allowed to end her days in peace at the home of her son-in-law, John Claypole, at Northborough Manor where she died in 1655. Thus the pamphleteers vigorously dipped their pens in "nothing but . . . the most biting sharpest ink". Elizabeth Cromwell was no stranger to slander. As her husband's influence increased so did the number of royalist libels, squibs and lampoons directed against Oliver and Elizabeth. As early as 1648 she was accused of aping the monarchy, in *The Cuckoo's Nest at Westminster*: "thou a Queen, a Brewer's wife a Queen; that Kingdom must needs be full of Drunkards when the King is a Brewer?" By 1650, in *News from the New Exchange,* royalist scribblers reached a new low in their rank obscenity, claiming that she "hath run through most of the regiment, both officers and soldiers. Since her coming

Caricature of Elizabeth Cromwell that appeared on the Frontispiece in "The Court and Kitchin of Elizabeth Cromwell" in 1664

into England (from Ireland) she hath traded never a jot the lesse in the low-countries". Within four years she was to be infamous, in the eyes of pamphleteers, as the niggardly "Protectress Joan". ❦ Elizabeth Cromwell remained all her life in the shadow of her husband's glory. The daughter of Sir James Bourchier, a prosperous fur-dealer and leather-dresser, she married Oliver in 1620. We have no depictions or descriptions of the young bride, however, and the most common representation is shown wearing plain clothes and clapped in her hood "like a Baggage Lady". ❦ A corrective is offered on examining Samuel Cooper's charming miniature of 1651 (see p. 19) showing a more fashionable lady with a hint of amusement in her face. A look of contentment might also be seen for, after thirty years of marriage, Oliver and Elizabeth could rest easy in their mutual devotion, as seen in Oliver's letter written immediately after smashing the Scots at Dunbar in September 1650: "Thou art dearer to me than any creature". Elizabeth, for her part, could chide him for sending only one letter to her three. ❡ The accusations of bribery, corruption and the amassing of plunder levelled at Elizabeth while she kept house at Drury Lane and the Cockpit lodgings are difficult to substantiate or rebut for the lack of evidence. Following the move to Whitehall in April 1654, however, we are on surer ground, largely thanks to Roy Sherwood's work on *The Court of Oliver Cromwell* (London, 1977). The author of "The Court and Kitchin" ascribes too much authority to the Protectoress in the running of the court. True, she made initiatives in the initial fitting out of the palace of Whitehall, but there is no evidence for the partitions, labyrinths, or trapdoors, let alone for her industry in pasturing cows in St. James Park, running a dairy, or employing six virtuous spinsters, nor did she check the Steward's accounts. Nor are the author's allegations of mass evictions at Whitehall borne out by the evidence even though there was a squatting problem at Hampton Court. The most notable fancy is the supposed performance of Mr. Starkey, the drunken cook, when summoned to appear before Oliver. Philip Starkey was employed as a master cook in Cromwell's household but there is no evidence for the incident nor for his dismissal. Indeed, he officiated at many entertainments for foreign ambassadors, his fee being £20. He was described by Samuel Pepys as "a great cook" and in 1668 became Master of the Company of Cooks. Such shameful conduct must be an invention of an over-worked imagination. The author is on steady ground, however, in his accurate description of the annual household expenses and his description of exact accounting and the absence of corruption. Little patronage was conferred or corruption permitted at the court of Oliver Cromwell. ❡ The main burden of complaint against Elizabeth Cromwell concerned her housekeeping. Undoubtedly she was of a thrifty nature – she had to be during her early married life at Huntingdon and St. Ives before Oliver became a man of property on inheriting his uncle's estate at Ely in 1638. At the palace of Whitehall she had her privy kitchen but the rest of the household was not hers to manage – that was the job of John Maidstone, Nathaniel Waterhouse, and Colonel Philip Jones, all members of Parliament. Moderation undoubtedly prevailed at Oliver's

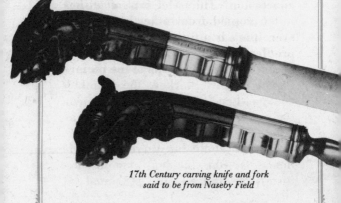

17th Century carving knife and fork said to be from Naseby Field

private table where "very rarely, or never, were our French *quelque choses* suffered by him, or any such modern gustos". Ill-health was the reason why Oliver's diet was "spare not curious". The family fastings were a testament to the religious beliefs of the Lord Protector and his Lady. Yet, although three Dutch envoys might be wined, dined and treated to a sung Psalm, the wedding of Oliver's youngest daughter, Frances, to the grandson of the Earl of Warwick, in November 1657, was celebrated with a banquet, the music of 48 violins and 50 trumpets, and mixed dancing until five in the morning – and Elizabeth Cromwell was not afraid to tread the boards with the royalist Earl of Newport. One should also note that in January 1657 a licence was issued for the purchase of 17,640 wine gallons of French and Spanish wines for the coming year. ❧ When we turn to the recipes offered by the author of "The Court and Kitchin" it is difficult to agree that they are "most of them ordinary and vulgar, except some few rarities". Comparison with contemporary cookbooks leads to a quite different conclusion. The selection of dishes (often copied from other volumes of "receipts") is a little odd in that there are few salads, pickles, sauces and confits, while two thirds of the recipes

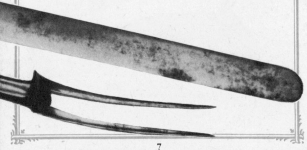

are devoted to meat, poultry, game and fish. Perhaps, unwittingly, the author has chosen to reflect the lack of balance in mid-seventeenth century diet – a heavy reliance on proteins and a comparatively low content of vegetable and fruit. We do see commonplace dishes of broth, oysters, and offal such as the country-style sausages but simple food accorded with Oliver's requirements and no banquet would be disgraced by the rare fricassee, venison pasty, or baked pig according to court fashion. It is left to the reader to follow the author's suggestion "to peruse the cookery" and perhaps to put into practise the recipes of Elizabeth Cromwell.

Douglas Clinton
Curator, Hinchingbrooke House

To help with reading the preliminary text of this book, difficult words or words that have changed their meaning have been printed in italic and are defined at the foot of the page. ❡ Notes have been provided where more explanation is required and these will be found on pages 91–96. They are signalled in the text by extra bold type and a small superior number. ❡ In the recipe section unfamiliar ingredients, equipment and methods are printed in italic and explanations for these terms will be found in the Glossary on pages 85–90.

TO THE READER

*T*hat there may no prejudice lie against this publication as an insultory, unmanlike invective and triumph over the supposed miserable and forlorn estate of this family, and this Person in particular, it will be requisite to obviate and prepare against that seeming humane (but indeed disloyal, or at least idle) sentiment and reverence to the frail and fluctuating condition of mankind, which as a general argument is ready at hand to oppose the design of the ensuing Treatise. ⁋ Not to refer the Reader to the practice of all times which have not failed to wreak the fury of the pen upon tyrants and usurpers (if surviving to punishment, otherwise their relations and posterity) whose execrable tragedies have wearied the world and blunted the instruments of death and slaughter, nor to instance the particular examples thereof as sufficient authority for this imitation; the *peculiar* justice due to the monstrous enormities and unparalleled insolence of these upstarts, besides the disproportion and incompetence of any revenge to their provoking impudent personation of princes, will *interestedly* vindicate and defend the author from the breach of charity much more from the rigid *imputation* and charge as of a person divested and void of nature, compassion and civility. ⁋ For while

peculiar: special; *interestedly:* repay with interest; *imputation:* accusation

9

they yet wanton in the abundance of their spoil and rapine, afflicted with nothing else but the torments of ambitious designs, taking this cloud upon them but as an eclipse of their former greatness and as but a turn of sporting fortune whose wheel may with an imaginary *volutation* roll their pretty Highnesses upwards again, how can the desperate depressed estate of many thousand loyal subjects who are irrecoverably lost and past all means but a miracle to their just, or any competent restitution, or to buoy up themselves or families from vulgar or fanatic contempt, how is it possible for them to *comport with* the serenity (instead of disaster) of this family, by whose single accursed plots and designs all their present and many more grievous past miseries are *derived* upon them and their posterity. ❡ And that this may not seem the froth and spleen of a satire, what meaneth that bleating in their present stately mansions? The same ceremonious and respectful observances as if they were still the *"Hogen Mogens"*. ❡ None of the family must presume to speak less than "My Lord" and "My Lady" to the **Squire Henry**[1] and his spouse and the same style is used whenever any mention is made of them in the household; to which *pin* the neighbours and necessary retainers addresses are tunably raised. What is this but to strengthen their weak yet vain-glorious fancy, and to preserve some relics of their former veneration, lest rude and inofficious time should plead a *disuser in bar* to their conceited (but airy) reversion? And no question but the old Gentlewoman, who took so much upon her and was so well pleased with her last grandeur as displeased and afflicted with the fall of it, betwixt **FLEETWOOD, RICHARD AND DESBOROUGH**[(2)] is also served in the same

Richard Cromwell, eldest surviving son of Oliver Cromwell. From a painting in the Cromwell Museum

manner and with the same *Grandezzas,* so that such is the inveterate itch and *tetter* of honour in her that nothing but the lees of gall and the most biting sharpest ink will ere be able to cure or stop this Protectorian evil. ¶ And herein we do but retaliate (if they be not unworthy of such a term, as that any attribute of justice should be profaned by their demerit, which exacts rather popular fury) and repay them in some sort those many libels, blasphemous pamphlets and *pasquils broached* and set on foot chiefly by the late usurper

volutation: turn; *comport with:* put up with; *derived:* descended; *"Hogen Mogens":* High Mightinesses (Dutch word for the Council of State of the Netherlands); *pin:* tuning peg of a stringed instrument; *disuser in bar:* legal term meaning disuse after lapse of time; *Grandezzas:* grandeur; *tetter:* any irritating skin disease; *pasquils:* lampoons or personal satires, usually posted up in a public place; *broached:* started off against the blessed memory and honour of our two late sovereigns; more especially those vile and impious pieces called "The court and character of King James" and "The Nonesuch Charles" (a great number of which were bought up in the juncture of the late **Restitution**[3] as particularly informed, which in the worst of times their bold and impudent falsehood made most abominable) were none of the least incentives to a work of this nature, in requital of that traitorous and most *petulant* imposture. ⁋ Whereas the guilt of this Grand-dame hath this sort of felicity, that it cannot be made worse or more odious by any additions of devised untruths; and he must be a very immodest and immoderate *fabulist* that can represent her to a greater disadvantage in this way than her actions have infamed her to the world. ⁋ Her Highness must be pleased to dispense with this frank and libertine manner of treating her, for 'tis all we are like to have for many millions, besides an old saw or proverb to the bargain: ⁋ **"Olim haec meminisse juvabit"**[4], a little transitory mirth for twenty years duration of sorrow; and if she thinks she comes not very well off so, she is as unreasonable in her reduction and allowed recess (to be envied for its plenty and amplitude, far exceeding her former *privacy*, so that she is even yet a darling of fortune) as in her usurped estate and greatness. ⁋ It is well for her if his butchery, than which the sun never saw a more *flagitious* execrable fact, and so comprehensive, that it reached **Caligula's**[5] wish, can be *sleighted* into her cookery and that there were no other monument of it than in paste. ℂ. **"Ut tantum schombros metuentia crimina, vel thus"** (6): That the records of his crimes were only damned to an oven. Little satisfaction serves the English nation (the relations of those loyal persons martyred by him excepted) and she ought therefore to be highly thankful that the scene of his tyranny was laid here, for had it *light* upon the Southern parts of the world their nimble and vindictive rage, upon the turn, would have *limbed* and minced her family to atoms, and have been their own cooks and carvers. ℂ. **Lambert Simnel** (7) very contentedly turned a *broach* in the king's kitchen after the *gaudies* of his kingly imposture, in the beginning of the reign of Henry the VII, and therefore for variety sake let this once mighty lady do drudgery to the public.

petulant: insolent; *fabulist:* one who invents falsehoods; *privacy:* meaning uncertain, may be either "private life" or "privation" i.e. poverty; *flagitious:* infamous; *sleighted:* thrown contemptuously; *light:* alighted; *limbed:* dismembered; *broach:* a spit for roasting meat; *gaudies:* showy celebrations; *Vale:* farewell

VALE

From a miniature by Samuel Cooper

THE INTRODUCTION

*A*mong all the monstrous effects of CROMWELL'S tyranny and the fruition of his usurped greatness, in the *affluence* of all imaginary delights to gratify his sense and *candy over* the troubles of his mind (to the rendering them less severe and dulling their poignant acuteness) it was by all men much wondered at that he was so little guilty of any luxurious and epicurean excesses either in his meat or drink, except sometimes in his cups, which he purposely and liberally took of to void the gravel in his kidneys, with which he was continually molested and for which large draughts were his ordinary cure. ⁋ In this he differed from the rest of his sanguineous tribe and sort of men who, making use of human blood for their drink, do *saginate* and fatten themselves with the superfluous variety of meats, to whose natural satisfaction such artificial devices are added (even re-torturing the creature) that the genuine *gusto* is quite changed by this adulteration and lost in the mixed multiplicity of other relishes and palatable ingredients. Herein like themselves, when not content with their natural private condition of life and the pure results and simple innocent delights thereof, they do corrode their minds with the sharp sauces of Ambi-

affluence: coming together; *candy over:* gloss over; *saginate:* fatten (animals); *gusto:* taste;

tion and so alter and invert their nature that they degenerate to other things and become such a **"quelque-chose"**[8] of villainy and debauchery that we can hardly *sever* and distinguish a crime which is not *intervitiated* with many [an] other. And what prodigious infamy upon this *gulose* and intemperate account, and by this very apt similitude, doth this day stick upon many if not most of the Roman Emperors! as I could instance in Tiberius, Caligula, Nero, Otho, Domitian, Commodus, Caracalla, Heliogabolus; men not to be mentioned without horror at their wickedness, of such savage and *feral* manners as if their food had been the flesh of panthers, tigers and bears and had assimilated its nutriment in their bestial qualities. But as was said before, Cromwell, as in some other cases, was in this wholly discriminated from them. ❡ Yet do I not think this abstemiousness and temperance was due only to his disposition either of body or mind, for his appetite in all other things was very irregular and inordinate, but either [sic:– "rather"?] to the multitude of those **"mordaces and edaces curae"**, biting and **eating cares**[9] and ambitious thoughts, which made him either the vultures or Tantalus his feast

Oliver Cromwell, etched by P. S. Lamborn from an original by Samuel Cooper

and were his continual surfeits of an evil conscience.

"Districtus ensis qui super impia Cervice pendet, non Siculae dapes Dulcem elaborarint saporem".[10]

Horace. "Ode".

Oliver Cromwell at Ripley Castle, etched by G. Wolliscroft Rhead from a painting by Rudolf Lehmann

❡ **Though I may indulge his military labours and discipline and example that severer abstinence: or else, which is principally intended here as the subject matter of this discourse, it may be cheaplier referred to the sordid frugality and thrifty baseness of his wife, Elizabeth Bowcher**[11]**, the daughter of Sir James Bowcher, commonly called "Protectoress Joan"**[12]** and vulgarly known of latter years by no other Christian name, even in the greatest height of her husband's power, and that chiefly out of derision and**

sever: separate; *intervitiated:* corrupted; *gulose:* greedy; *feral:* bestial

contemptuous indignation that such a person durst presume to take upon herself such a sovereign estate when she was a hundred times fitter for a barn than a palace. So sporting, mocking Fate, to make good that of the satirist **"Felix a tergo quem nulla ciconia pinxit"**,[13] followed her great luck with that sarcastic and *dicterious* nickname, that she with her *Copemate* might perceive their fortune was not so entire and of so fair an aspect and firm structure, but that the flaws and blemishes and impotence thereof were most obvious and ridiculous. Their fine feathers had swans feet and their beautiful *mermaid,* the fiction of dominion, had the ugly tail and fins of a fish. ℂ The train of her greatness and prosperity was the most vile and scornful reproaches. And this shall suffice to be spoken of her person by way of Preface; the next *elenchus* or discourse is of her *mesnagery,* housewifery or housekeeping.

dicterious: witty; *Copemate:* a partner in power, an accomplice in cheating; *mermaid:* a symbol of corrupt power; *elenchus:* cross-examination – method used by Socrates, of eliciting truth by means of short question and answer; *mesnagery:* management

THE

COURT AND KITCHEN

OF

Elizabeth Cromwell from miniature
by Samuel Cooper. Reproduced by kind permission of
BBC Hulton Picture Library

MRS. ELIZABETH[14]

alias

JOANE CROMWELL

*T*o confine and limit this treatise to its purpose and designment prefixed in the title, we must (though with some petty injury to the reader) pass over her economy at her private home, before Oliver's bold achievement and attainment of the supreme power (because part of it is already public) when she had brought, as we say *"a noble to ninepence"* by her pious negligence and ill management of the domestic affairs, and was as *giddy* to see her bare walls as Oliver was mad with enthusiasms and divinations of regal furniture and all princely pomp and greatness. Those memorials may be reduced to this present use in this short *corollary*. ❡ "That the former extremities of her necessitous and indigent condition, upon the bettering thereof (by the general ruin) raised in her such a *quick* sense of the misery of want that she became most industriously provident and resolvedly sparing and cautious for the future, and to prefer the certainty of her own care and diligence to the extempore, fond and easy delusions of **"Deus providebit"**[15], with which she had been fooled before into an almost voluntary and devoted poverty". ❡ This her aspect and consideration of the future extended itself (with more prudence and sagacity than her husband would descend to) on some humble thoughts of her present rise levelled to her past depression. She took a prophetical prospect of the times and having seen two, three or four variations in the calmness and tranquillity of her husband's fortunes, did wisely *presage* to herself that after those hurly-burlies of war and the tempest of rebellion, wherein he had whirled, and with so much impatient precipitancy engaged himself, there would another turn happen, against which she concluded to be more differently armed. ❡ The first eddy of that boisterous and unruly current of his prosperity, which at last over-ran all banks and boundaries, flowed into the receptacle of her committeeship in the affected counties, particularly Cambridge and Huntingdon, where to recover and piece up her ruins she, with the same spirit of zeal and piety of her husband's, consecrated her house to be the Temple of Rapine, one of the prime goddesses next the Cause; whither for sacrifices all manner of

*Oliver Cromwell, engraving
by Francis Holl from a painting by Van Dyke*

cattle, clean and unclean, were brought from all the adjacent parts, as [were] other costly utensils of the best moveables, to adorn and enrich this sacred place; from whence to hope for any re-delivery was mental sacrilege and to endeavour it was punished with irreparable ruin. And I am sure (like the guilt of that crime) there are some who now feel it to the third generation, and may without miracle to perpetuity. ❡ For not only was her *corban* to be satisfied with the product of such *oblations*, but lands were to be set apart and *sequestred*, the revenue of which passed first through her fingers and were made *impropriations* of her own. ❡ Having thus recruited her estate and adjusted her present seizures to her past losses, and exalted above the dignity of Mrs. Sheriff, or Countess of those shires, no person her equal in greatness. Upon the success of her husband after **Marston Moor**(16) she abandoned the dull country, partly not enduring the ordinary demeanour of her acquaintances towards her, nor sufferable nor endurable by her betters for her imperious and unsociable carriage towards all persons of quality, and partly to partake in the supreme fruition of the City's more elaborate and exquisite pleasures and to housewife early admiration: for the ladies of the Cause began to appear at Thanksgiving dinners and to reckon as many dishes to a *mess* as their husbands numbered achievements. ❡ At her arrival in town she was little less than saluted by the whole *Juncto*, though not in a body, yet severally by them all, and afterwards by the pastors, elders and brethren of the sects, who came not a-housewarming with the breath of their mouths in zealous congratulations, but brought all silver implements for her accommodation of household stuff, and offered them according to the late pattern of Reformation in Guildhall. Nor did this humour cease here. The middle sort of the religiously fanatic sent her in Westphalia hams, *neats tongues, puncheons* and *tierces* of French wine, *runlets* and bottles of *sack*, all manner of preserves and *comfits* to save her the trouble of the town. The most of which gifts, they being multiplied upon her, she retailed by private hands at as good a rate as the market would afford. ❡ But much more of these was given afterwards when Oliver was returned from the ending [of] the war, and was looked upon as the great motion of the

Parliament's proceedings. Not to reckon those immoderate bribes that obtruded themselves upon her, more welcome by far than those saintlike benevolences and civil offices of love, under which their corrupting practices were veiled to no purpose, for she very well understood the very first addresses though never so innocently remote from the main design, and would rate them as they do *post miles* (for she kept her constant distant stages in all her public brokerage and transactions) duly and exact.

⁋ And indeed her house was in this respect a political or state Exchange by which the affairs of the kingdom were governed and the prices of all things set, whether offices, preferments, indemnity, as all other manner of collusion and deceits were practised and money stirring nowhere else. And in the other respect of provisions, it might have passed for the Temple of **"Bel and the Dragon"**[17] (to pursue the former sanctity of her rural mansions) where all those offerings of diet were consumed, or as good, altered and assimilated to her nature (the use of the nutritive faculty) by serving her covetousness in their reduction to money. Now she needed no such austere diligence in the preservation of an estate, for it was more than she and her ministers could do to receive it. It was impossible to keep any decorum or order in that house, where masterless money like a haunting spirit possessed and disquieted every room. It was a kind of Midas his palace, where there was nothing but gold to eat, only instead of being confined to that indigestible food she and her servants were most frequently invited

corban: church treasury (used here ironically); *oblations:* offerings to God; *sequestred:* confiscated (usually forcibly); *impropriations:* annexed church properties, the income from which was kept for personal use; *mess:* meal; *Juncto:* a self-elected committee or council, usually of a political character; *neats tongues:* ox or bullock's tongues; *puncheons:* large casks varying in capacity from 72 gallons (beer) to 120 gallons (whisky); *tierces:* measure of capacity, varying for different commodities, for wine it was usually 42 gallons. *runlets:* cask or vessel varying between 18½ gallons and one pint; *sack:* white wine, imported from Spain and the Canaries; *comfits:* sweetmeats, usually caraway seeds or almond nuts covered in sugar; *post miles:* stages along a post-road or posting route, as used by mail coaches out of doors to most sumptuous and magnificent treatments, whence because of that more sacred employment at home (like Sabbatarians that provide themselves baked and cold meats for the superstitious observation of the day) they and their *progging* lady brought home such relics as they might *mumble down* in the dispatch of their business and save the trouble or magic of their long graces, which had brought a curse instead of a blessing upon their masters and mistresses first endeavours. Though she herself — so hard it is to forego and shake off an habitual customary hypocrisy and fallacy — would look as religiously upon a *marchpane*, preserve, or comfit as a despairing lover upon his mistress's lips. ⁊ But the war expired, and those thanksgiving and triumphal festivals over and ended, this pious family began to enter upon the years of famine after those of plenty. Her husband was now engaged in deep designs and practices upon the King and Kingdom, and, in order to ruin them both, upon the Army. Every one of those mischievous and *Machiavellian* consultations and projects were ushered continually by a fast, which being appointed for and observed by the host were always intimated to the friends and relations of the officers and kept by them with no less strictness in their private households; which by the frequent shifts and various turns of policy, which Cromwell's fate and the uncertainty of the times guided him to, came so often and thick upon the neck of one another that her domestics had almost forgot dinner time; upstart Piety, like the modern Frugality, *bating* a meal, and as that had limited the diet to noon, this changed it and diverted it to night. ⁊ So that, as in other authoritative continued fasts there is a political and humane reason, viz, the sparing the creature, even to the same end this good housewife directed her domestic abstinence; and when on such occasions she had cause to suspect a general discontent of her people and household, she would up with this Scripture expression and lay it on their teeth for better fare: "The Kingdom of God is not meat and drink, but righteousness and peace", and some such Scriptural *dehortations* from gluttony and the like luxurious intemperance, and other zealous sentences of moderation in diet: as, that the pleasure of a full diet consists more in desire than in satiety; that to have the stomach twice repleted in the day is to empty the brain and to render the mind unserviceable to the actions of life; no abyss, no whirlpool is so pernicious as gluttony, which the more a man eats makes him more a-hungry; and the better he dines to sup the worse, with other such morals taken out of **"Gusman"**[18] and **"Lazarillo de Tormes"**[19] and only altered a little by being made serious in practice. ❡ Yet I cannot pass this necessary lesson of Temperance, however it proceeds from this *sophistical* corrupt teacher thereof, without some reflection on some more ancient and authentic instructions. But because it is a little beside my design I will conclude them in some fit sentences, as of the satirist Persius.

"Poscis opem nervis corpusque
  fidele senecta,
Esto age: sed grandes patinae
  tucetaque crassa,
Annuere his superos vetuere Jovemque
  morantur".

Englished thus, by **De Barten Holyday.**[20]

"Thou wishest for firm nerves, and for a sure sound body, that would healthfully endure until old age; why be it, that thy wish is granted by the Gods; yet thy large dish
And full fat sausage make the Gods delay
To bless thee, and do force good Jove to stay".[21] ❡ And that other of Epitectus, worthy to be inscribed in all our parlours and banqueting-houses Σωφροσυνην λεγεσθαι ὡς σωζωσαν την φρόνησιν. Καὶ αὐτην ψυχην εἶναι σοφωτατην.[22]

---

progging: foraging ("prog" was a vulgar word for food especially provisions for a journey or excursion); *mumble down:* chew without making much use of the teeth; *march-pane:* marzipan; *Machiavellian:* unscrupulous (particularly in politics), from the name of Niccolo Machiavelli (1469–1527) a Florentine statesman who held that terrorism and deceit were justifiable in some political circumstances; *bating:* abating; *dehortations:* earnest dissuasions; *sophistical:* employing arguments which are intentionally deceptive.

❡ In another place, **"Inter epulandum duos excipere debemus convivas, corpus et animam. Tum quod in corpus collatum fit repente effluxurum, quod autem in animam perpetuo servandum"** (i.e.) in feasting and banquetting we must except two guests the body and the mind, because that which is bestowed on the body will suddenly pass away, and that which comes into the mind will be there laid up for ever[23]; adding that commendation of Plato to a friend, a philosopher; **"Vestrae quidem cenae non solum in praesentia sed etiam postero die sunt iucundae"**[24], intimating that there is no such lasting pleasure as in a sober diet, which, when excesses bring surfeits, renews the feast the next day, and gives a continual relish to the appetite.

❡ But I must beg pardon for this otherwise seasonable digression and reduce the discourse in pursuit of her Ladyship's errantry from one abode to another in the suburbs of London, more or less like a *sojourner* (however she inhabited whole houses) and a great person incognito than as a woman of that state and degree to which her husband's condition and command and great probabilities of succeeding titles, did forespeak her. If any thing could be observable by her for state and charge, it was the keeping of a coach, the driver of which served her for caterer, as much occasion as she had for him, for butler, for serving man, for gentleman-usher when she was to appear in any public place. And this coach was bought at the secondhand out of a great number which then lay by the walls, while their honourable owners went on foot and ambled in the dirt to Goldsmiths and Haberdashers Halls, if so fairly come by. She might, and she did ('twas thought) save that very inconsiderable charge, but the sense she had how obvious and odious her carriage in a *sequestered caroach* would be to everybody made her jealous of such scorn and derision. As for horses, she had them out of the Army, and the stabling and livery in her husband's allotment out of the Mews, at the charge of the State; so that it was the most thrifty and unexpensive pleasure and divertissement, besides the finery and honour of it, that could be imagined; for it saved many a meal at home, when upon pretence of business, her ladyship went abroad, and carrying some dainty *provant* for her own and her daughters own repast, she spent the whole day in short visits and long walks in the air, so that she seemed to affect the *Scythian* fashion, who dwell in carts and wagons and have no other habitations. ❦ Her public retinue was also very slender and as slenderly *accoutred,* no more, commonly, than one of her husband's horse boys running by her, sometimes one and sometimes another; with or without livery, all was one; on purpose, it may be well supposed, beside the saving of the cost, to prevent her being discried and discovered, so much suspicion and hatred had her husband drawn upon himself, even from the *vulgar,* which she feared might by some such badge of notice light upon herself in the streets as she passed. ❦ She was the same recluse likewise in her habit, rather harnessing herself in the defence of her clothes than allowing herself the loose and open bravery thereof, as not having been used to such "light armour". And her hood, till her face was seen in her Highnesses glass, was clapped on like a *headpiece,* without the art of *ensconcing* and *entrenching* it double and single in *"redoubts"* and *"hornworks".* In fine, she was *"cap-a-pie"* like a baggage lady and was out of her element in her vicinity to the Court and City. ❦ But her daughters were otherwise vested and robed, and a constant expense allowed in *'tire-women,* perfumers and the like arts of gallantry, with each their maid and servant to attend them; and by their array and deportment their quality might have been guessed at. They were all (those that were unmarried) very young but **Mrs. Elizabeth**[25], who about this time was married to one **Mr. Claypole's son**[26] of Northamptonshire (the old man having had a

---

sojourner: a temporary resident: *sequestred:* confiscated; *caroach:* a stately or luxurious coach for town use; *provant:* provisions; *Scythian:* gipsy, from Scythia, an ancient region of Russia inhabitated by nomadic people; *accoutred:* dressed; *vulgar:* common people; *headpiece:* hat; *ensconcing, entrenching, "redoubts", "hornworks":* all military terms used mockingly to draw attention to Mrs. Cromwell's lack of interest in her appearance; *"cap-a-pie":* head to foot; *tire-women:* dressmakers

Elizabeth Claypole, favourite daughter of Oliver Cromwell and her home Northborough Castle, near Peterborough

hand in the same disloyal service with Oliver in that county) but with a very private wedding no way suitable to that pomp and grandeur which Oliver kept in the Army, where he was looked upon with the same reverence and respect as the General himself. All that was *"Hymen-like"* in the celebration of it was some freaks and pranks, without the aid and company of a fiddler (which in those days was thought by their precise parents to be altogether unlawful and favouring of carnality, as the ring and form of marriage were thought superstitious and anti-Christian) in *Nol's* military rude way of spoiling of the custard and, like *"Jack Pudding"* throwing it upon one another; which was ended in the more manly game of buffeting with cushions and flinging them up and down the room. ❧ Neither appeared there the splendour and ornament of jewels and pearls and the like lustre of gems, whose individious refractions like poisonous *effluxes* might envenom the world with spleen and malice at their plundered and stolen radiancy. For by the manifold surrenders and stormings of houses and castles Cromwell had amassed good store of rarities, besides medals, and gold and silver vessels (the spoils of our captivity) which it was not as yet safe to produce in such an unsettlement of his conquest, till all property should be huddled up in the general ruin; out of whose mixed and confused rubbish, in his new polished Government they might exert their brightness *underivable* and clear from all former title and claim; as the mass of things shall be *mell* and *calcined* together at the last universal dissolution. ❧ And I have heard it reported for a truth that most of the precious moveables and other things of value, at the storming of **Basing House**[(27)] by Cromwell, fell into his hands either immediately or directly, the soldiers either by command or for some small price returning several precious pieces of the spoil, whose worth they understood not, to his agents, who gave an exact account thereof to the Lady Receiver at home, who was about that time seen to be very pleasant and *prajeant* at the enjoyment of those pretty things, as she expressed herself, being the best for substance and ornament that belonged to the noble Marquess of Winchester and his family, which this she-usurper now listed and catalogued for her own. ❧ And if the whole inventory of her rapinous hoard were now producible, what a voracious monster would she appear to be? Not a corner in the Kingdom which is not sensible of her ravage and which had not a share in the *Lombard* of her uncountable and numberless chattels. ❧ How

❧

Hymen-like: marriage-like, 'Hymen' was the Greek and Roman god of marriage; *Nol's:* Oliver's; *"Jack Pudding":* a buffoon and companion of a charlatan who frequently engaged in slapstick comedy; *effluxes:* out flowings; *underivable:* unidentifiable; *mell:* mixed; *calcined:* reduced to ashes; *prajeant:* swaggering; *Lombard:* a play upon words — "Lombard" is a name for a pawnbroker or pawnshop and also a culinary term, "Lombard pie" or "Lumber pie", which was a savoury pie made of meat or fish and eggs.

many rare pieces of antique gold and silver are again damned to the earth from whence they were brought and are by her mischievous covetousness irrecoverably lost, which have been the glories and monumental pride of many families? and the only remains and evidences of their noble hospitality now buried by this wretch in hugger-mugger? ¶ Those advantages, together with the *vails* of the Army, which she had upon every commission and other incident occasions, for her husband's interests and authority, together with his extraordinary pay and the appurtenances to it, and lands and *hereditaments* bestowed on him, besides rewards and gratuities in ready money, amounted to an incredible sum which almost glutted her eyes to satiety, but so, that they were yet lesser than her belly, which could stow as much more with convenience enough, and conserve and secure it by a very parsimonious use and narrow strict disbursement; for having now quitted all fears of returning to a private condition by the insolence of her husband's fortunes, which drove at the sovereignty, and abominable design being communicated to her, this great bank was still kept supplied by her for the support and maintenance of that dignity and supremacy to which Oliver aspired, and to facilitate his way to it; having rightly perceived that nothing but money had carried on the war and brought things to that pass, whatever was pretended of zeal and to the Cause. And therefore there was no difference in her manner of housekeeping, only Cromwell being now in Town for the most part conspiring that execrable parricide against the King, she dispensed with her niggardly regulation, and having taken a house near Charing Cross kept it in a manner open for all comers, which were none but the Sectary party and Officers, who resorted thither as to their headquarters with all their wild projections, and were entertained with *small beer* and bread and butter, which to the animation of the approaching villainy was as bad as *"Aqua fortis"* and horseflesh. For as was said of Caesar, **"Nemo tam sobrious ad Republicam evertendam accessit"** – "No man came more sober to the destruction of the Commonwealth"[(28)]; so I may aptly and more justly say, That no men of more abstemiousness ever effected so vile and *flagitious* an enterprise upon so just a Government. ❡ That being in *perpetration*, Mrs. Cromwell ran out of purse some score of pounds (for it is to be remembered that she stewarded it all along, Oliver's head being busy with greater and worser matters) very much to her regret and vexation. But that villainy over, and some two or three private treatments given his most sure and addicted accomplices in exaltation of their monstrous success, the doors of the house were again barred, and all persons hindered and of difficult admittance upon what score or business so ever; and now she was returned to her former privacy and ordinary diet as before. ❡ During the rest of the time while Cromwell stayed in England she kept the same tenor, having received (besides a confirmation of the Marquess of Worcester's estate to the value of five thousand pounds a year) upon the account of the defeat given the **Levellers**[(29)] by her husband's treachery, at a Thanksgiving dinner (whereto he was invited by the City) a piece of gold plate of very good value, which discharged the former expense. ❡ I must admit many other passages during his absence in Ireland and in Scotland, and after this *liminary* but *prolix* account sum up all in her menage of her

vails: casual or occasional profits; *hereditaments:* property that could be inherited;
small beer: beer of weak, poor or inferior quality;
Aqua fortis: commercial nitric acid (HNO_2), a powerful solvent and corrosive; *flagitious:* infamous; *perpetration:* the act of committing a crime or an offence; *liminary:* preliminary.
prolix: long and wordy

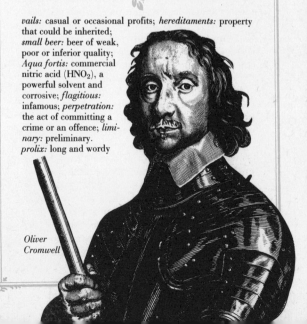

Oliver Cromwell

domestic affairs at Whitehall, for which she had so long prepared and furnished herself with Rules of Government and Economy fitted for her usurpation and the times. ⁋ For her husband brought not so great and haughty, as she base and low spirited thoughts and resolutions to the grandeur of that place, the habitation and residence of the greatest and most famous monarchs of the world, and famed throughout it for truly royal and princely pomp and immense munificence and entertainment. ⁋ She had flesh enough indeed to become any room in that spacious mansion, but so little of a brave spirit that the least hole of it would have made her a banquetting house; but like a spirit she came only to haunt, not to enjoy any part of it. The *Penates and Genii* of the place abominating this profane and sacrilegious intrusion neither giving him one hour's quiet or rest in it from his troubled, mistrustful and ill-boding thoughts, nor her any content and satisfaction but what she found in repining and vexing herself at the cost and charge the maintenance of that beggarly court did every day put her to. ⁋ It was in the year 1653 that Cromwell first possessed and seated himself there as in his own right and in chief, and brought his worshipful family thither to their several apartments, she having appointed one Mr. Maidstone to be Steward of his house and one Mr. Starkey to be his Master Cook, who afterwards was betrayed and taken drunk in his cellar (designing the like upon my Lord Mayor's sword-bearer while my Lord was in conference with the Protector) so that he could not conceal it from the household; who, out of spite to him as being a spy over their actions and behaviours, first acquainted their Lady, and she Oliver, with the fault, aggravated by the scandal and wasteful excess; insomuch that Starkey was commanded to come before him, where instead of a compliment and excuse he delivered himself by vomit in the very face of his master and was thereupon dismissed the house. ⁋ It will not be too distant a review to observe and remark her introduction to and *seizin* of this royal mansion (which we have only mentioned) before any other procedure in the economy thereof. ⁋ The first preparatory as to public notice was an Order from the new

Council of State after the Dissolution of the Parliament commanding all persons to depart out of Whitehall, which was then the den of a hundred several families and persons of power and office in the anarchy; which being difficultly and grumblingly executed, she herself employed a surveyor to make her some convenient accommodations and little labyrinths and trap stairs, by which she might at all times unseen pass to and fro and come unawares upon her servants and keep them vigilant in their places, and honest in the discharge thereof. ⁋ Several repairs were likewise made in her own apartments, and many small partitions up and down, as well above stairs as in the cellars and kitchens, so that it looked like the picture of **"Bartholomew Fair"**[(30)]. Her Highness-ship, not being yet accustomed to that roomy and august dwelling, and perhaps afraid of the vastness and silentness thereof, which presented to her thoughts the desolation her husband had caused, and the dreadful apparitions of those Princes whose *incensed* ghosts wandered up and down and did *attend* some avenging opportunity; and this was the more believable because she (not to name her husband's misgiving, suspicions and frights) could never endure any whispering or to be alone by herself in any of the chambers. ⁋ And it is further here fit to be instanced, that upon her first coming, when her harbingers had appointed her lodgings the same with the Queen's, which yet retained their royal names and distinctions, she would by no means hear of them but changed them into other appellations, that there might remain no manner of disgust and discontent to her ambitious and usurping greatness; and therefore they were adapted now into the like significations, by the name of the Protector's and Protectoress's Lodgings, as more proper and fitting terms to their propriety and indisputed possession. ⁋ Much ado she had at first to raise her mind and deportment to this sovereign

Penates and Genii: guardian spirits – in Roman mythology the "Penates" were the guardian deities of the household and were worshipped in the interior of every dwelling-house; *seizin:* possession; *incensed:* angry; *attend:* await.

grandeur; and very difficult it was for her to lay aside those impertinent meannesses of her private fortune; like the **bride-cat**[(31)] by Venus's favour metamorphosed into a comely virgin that could not forebear catching at mice, she could not *comport with* her present condi-

Elizabeth Cromwell, from a painting in the Cromwell Museum

tion nor forget the common converse and affairs of life; but like some kitchen maid preferred by the lust of some rich and noble dotard, was ashamed of her sudden and gaudy bravery, and for a while skulked up and down the house, till the fawning observances and reverences of her slaves had raised her to a confidence not long after sublimed into an impudence. ⵊ And this was helped on by Madam **Pride** and my Ladies **Hewson** and **Berkstead, Goff, Whalley**[(32)], etc., who all came to compliment her Highness upon the felicity of Cromwell's assumption to the government, and to congratulate her fortune and so accompany her to her Palace of Whitehall, where like the Devil cast out she entered by fasting and praying, after the usual manner, and like devout Jezebel took possession of Naboth's Vineyard. ❡ And thus we have waited on her to this *basilicon*, now swept and cleansed for her friendly entertainment; and the chimneys smoked and heated again which had suffered so long a damp and after so long a vacation. Especially her Highness took care and gave strict charge to have all the rooms aired, for fear of those ill scents **the Rump**[(33)] had left behind them, and was willing to be at the charge of perfumes to expel the noisomeness thereof, the account of which hath been seen by *divers*, allowed by her own hand; but foul odour was so equally natural to all the Grandees that Oliver when he died left it in a worse condition than when he found it, as is public in several treatises. ❡ Cromwell was now his own Steward and carver, not limited to any expenses of housekeeping no more than to the charges of the Government; but was absolute both at dinner and at Council board, neither of which were yet well settled. And therefore, besides the *nearness* of his wife, it was necessary he should appear extraordinary frugal of the people's purse (who wished every bit he eat might choke him, for all his temperance) in his private and public disbursements. Only that he might not appear so much a military governor, but have something of the Prince in him, about noon-time a man might hear a huge clattering of dishes and noise of servitors in rank and file marching to his table (though neither sumptuously nor extraordinarily furnished) in some imitation of Paulus Emilius in his answer to the Grecians after his triumph and conquest of Perseus, the last Macedon King; **"Eiusdem esse animi et aciem et convivium instruere, illam quidem ut formidulosus hostibus hoc ut amicis gratus appareat";** in English thus, "Tis of the same spirit to order a battle as to furnish a feast, by the one a man appears terrible to his enemies

---

comport with: put up with; *basilicon:* this is a mistake, the word should be "basilica" i.e. a royal palace; *divers:* many people; *nearness:* meanness.

and by the other pleasing to his friends".[34] ⁋ But at his private table, very rarely or never were our French **"quelque-choses"**[8] suffered by him, or by such modern *gusto's*, whether with the fright he was prejudiced of poison by such devices (at an invitation made him and his General the **Lord Fairfax**[35], with the other of the Supreme Commanders of the Army, by a small officer therein who was formerly a cook at a lady's in Hammersmith, where with one leg of mutton dressed all sorts of ways he entertained them all; but upon their discovery of the fellow's audaciousness in bidding them, which prompted them to believe it was a design against their lives and put most of them to the vomit, was like to have been dressed himself by the hangman) or by some stronger or more masculine appetite, which partaked with his other robust faculties, is uncertain; sure it is that when in treatments given his familiars such things were set upon the table "twas more for show and sport than for Belly Timber and about which the good housewife never troubled her head. ⁋ She, to return to her government, very providentially kept two or three cows in St. James's Park, and erected a new office of a dairy in Whitehall, with dairy maids to attend that business solely, (as most of the employment for servants was managed by females, for there were no Sergeants but such as waited with halberds on the Guard) and fell to the old trade of churning butter and making buttermilk; nor were **Oxford Kate's**[36] fine things half so famous among the Cavalier ladies as my Lady Protector's butter among the mushroom zealous ladies of the Court, most whereof being apple or oyster women, or stocking-heelers and the like did much wonder at and magnify the invention and rarity. ⁋ Next to this covey of milk maids she had another of *spinsters* and sewers, to the number of six, who sat the most part of the day, after she was ready, in her privy chamber sewing and stitching; they were all of them ministers' daughters, such as were inveterate Nonconformists to the Church, for which cause, and the pretence of piety (the main ingredient to things of the least moment) they were added to the family. Nor did the Turkish ministers take more care to furnish the seraglio and gratify their master with choice virginities than some of these pious pimps did lay out for indigent godly maidens to pleasure this prostitute charity of hers, that the world might take notice of her exemplary humility and compassion. But indeed all persons of breeding and quality abhorred the indignity of her service, and so rather than be served with common drudges she erected this new order and continued it to the term of her usurpation. Herein following the steps of her husband, who made a new daring militia of zealous persons since he could not be served with generous spirits. ⁋ She was once resolved by the assistance and advice of her mother to have made a small brewing place, with vessels and other accommodation for her own and Oliver's drink, as not liking the City brewing nor trusting to the artifices of the town; but about the same time a drink was then grown famous in London, being a very small ale of 7s. 6d. a barrel, well boiled and well tasted and conditioned, called and known by the name of "Morning Dew" (from the brewer's name as I have heard) which was thence brought into request at Court and was the cool refreshing entertainment of those bouncing Ladies that came weltering and wallowing in their coaches instead of drays to visit her. ⁋ And for the kitchen and pantry a great reformation was intended, but the multitude of comers and goers upon her first settling there, and numbers of mouths which came gaping for preferment, being to be stopped with victuals, put her besides her proposed regulation; yet was there not a joint of meat for which the cook was not to give an account, which she overlooked as it came from them to the steward, whose accounts likewise were punctually cast up by her and *'firmed* by her hand as well as afterwards by the Protector's. ⁋ Nay, so severe and strict she was in this thrifty way of housekeeping that she descended to the smallest and meanest matters, the very chaffer and price of the market, and that the reader may not think he is imposed on and deceived by a general imputation of her

gusto's: tastes; *spinsters:* used here in the original meaning of "one who spins"; *firmed:* confirmed.

your most humble servant
Oliver Cromwell

June 14ᵗʰ 1645.
Hausebuour.

Engraving by Francis Holl from a miniature by Samuel Cooper

niggardlyness I will give him two notable and apposite instances. ⁋ The first was the very next summer after his coming to the Protectorate in 1654, in June, at the very first season of green peas, where a poor country woman living somewhere about London having a very early but small quantity in her garden, was advised to gather them and carry them to the Lady Protectoress, her counsellors conceiving she would be very liberal in her reward, they being the first of that year. Accordingly the poor woman came to the Strand, and having her peas, amounting to a *peck* and a half, in a basket, a cook by the Savoy as she passed either seeing or guessing at them, demanded the price, and upon her silence offered her an *angel* for them. ⁋ But the woman expecting some greater matter went on in her way to Whitehall, where after much ado she was directed to her chamber, and one of her maids came out, and understanding it was a present and rarity, carried it to the Protectoress, who out of her princely munificence sent her a *crown*, which the maid *told* into her hand. The woman seeing this baseness and the frustration of her hopes, and remembering withal what the cook had proffered her, threw back the money into the maid's hands and desired her to fetch her back her peas, for that she was offered five shillings more for them before she brought them thither and could go fetch it presently; and so half slightingly and half ashamedly this great lady returned her present putting it off with a censure upon the unsatisfactory daintiness of luxurious and prodigal epicurism. The very same peas were afterwards sold by the woman to the said cook, who is yet alive to justify the truth of this relation. ⁋ The other is of a later date, upon Oliver's rupture with the Spaniard, the commodities of that country grew very scarce, and the prices of them raised by such as could procure them underhand. Among the rest of those goods the fruits of the growth of that place were very rare and dear, especially oranges and lemons. ⁋ One day, as the Protector was private at dinner, he called for an orange to a loin of veal, to which he used no other sauce, and urging the same command was answered by his wife that "Oranges were oranges now, that *crab oranges* would cost a *groat* and for her part she never intended to give it"; and it was presently whispered that sure her Highness was never the adviser of the Spanish War and that his Highness should have done well to have consulted his digestion before his hasty and inordinate appetite of dominion and riches in the West Indies. ⁋ I might confirm this

peck: measure of capacity for dry goods equal to 2 gallons (7½ litres); *angel:* an old English coin, value 10/- (50p); *crown:* gold coin, value 5/- (25p), first minted in 1526; *told:* counted; *crab oranges:* inferior, sour oranges; *groat:* a silver coin, value 4d (about 1½p).

by other *retrenchments* of expense, whensoever she could confine his table to her own privacy; particularly it was a great mode and taken up by his court party to roast half capons, pretending a more exquisite taste and nutriment in it than when dressed whole and entire; where I cannot but smile to think how it puzzled her Ladyship's carver to hold him to the knife and to apportion half and quarter limbs according to art. ❡ Much more do I wonder what those fellows at Rome did, or what they would have done here, who kept carving schools, **"ludi structorii"**[37], and had all manner of fowl and fish and such other grand festival meat carved in wood, which they marked out with wooden knives with very great curiosity, and instructed their scholars, who learned it was a worshipful employment and way to preferment, as the satirist very elegantly.

**Sumine cum magno lepus atque aper et Pygargus
Et Scythiae volucres, et Phoenicopterus ingens,
Et Gaetulus oryx hebeti lautissima ferro
Caeditur, et tota sonat ulmea cena Suburra.**

Englished thus:

"The sow's large teat, the hare and boar and deer, Scythian and Afric's fowl and bearded beast, The Gaudies of the town in wood appear, So with dull iron carved sounds elmy feast".[38] ❡ And if it were not made almost incredible by the superfluity and excess of her fortune, which cannot be supposed to have no way advanced her thoughts from her former industry and frugal care and *intendancy*, I might insert a story of her enquiry into the profit of the kitchen staff and the exchanging of it for candles, which those that knew her humour had purposely put into her head; till she was told to whom it belonged, and the customs of the Court, to most of which she answered, they should not think to have them take place as in "the other woman's" days, for she would look better to it; like Vespasian, she had learnt, that **"Dulcis odor lucri ex re qualibet"** – "Gain was sweet from whatever thing". ❧ And the reason she used to give for this her frugal inspection and parsimony was the small allowance and mean pittance she had to defray the household expenses, which at her first coming to Court-Keeping was barely sixty-four thousand pounds per annum; until **Colonel Philip Jones**[39] came to be Comptroller of the Household, when the weekly charge was Nineteen hundred twenty three pounds odd money, the *defalcation* of the rest, from the just sum of two thousand pounds, at the rate of £100,000 yearly, making up the four thousand pound for the two weeks above the 50. So exactly was this charge computed, and method punctually observed, that there might be no place for excess, and by means thereof for deceit or any colluding practices. ❧ Her order of eating and meal times was not less regulated, and though inverted, yet designed well to the decency as well as conveniency of her service. So, first of all, at the ringing of a bell dined the Halberdiers, or men of the Guard with the inferior officers; then the bell rung again and the Steward's table was set (in the same hall near the Water Stairs) for the better sort of those that waited on their Highnesses, ten of whom were apportioned to a table or mess, one of which was chosen by themselves every week for steward, and he gave the clerk of the kitchen the bill of fare as was agreed upon generally every morning.   To these ten men, and what friends should casually come to visit them, the value of 10 shillings in what flesh or fish soever they would have, with a bottle of sack and two of claret, was appointed; but to prevent after comers from expecting anything in the kitchen there was a general rule that if any man thought his business would detain him beyond dinner time he was to give notice to the steward of his Mess, who would set aside for him as much as his share came to and leave it in the buttery. ❧ Suppers likewise they had none, eggs or some *slops* contenting Cromwell and her Ladyship, and to his *exemplar* all was conformed. In

retrenchments: economies; *intendancy:* management; *defalcation:* deduction; *slops:* liquid or semi-liquid food, term used here contemptuously; *exemplar:* example;

lieu thereof, for the family there was constantly boiled 8 stone of beef early in the morning, to keep her retainers in heart and in *earnest* of a dinner, the broth whereof, and all the scraps and relics of dinner (to give her her due) were alternately given to the poor of Saint Margaret's Westminster and Saint Martin in the Fields, according to the Churchwarden's Roll of each parish; and that very orderly, without any brabble or noise; so that amidst so many curses and imprecations which were uttered against him he had some prayers and blessings from those hungry Jack Dawes that frequented and attended this dole. But those lame, decrepit and starved precepts never reached halfway, and like impotent suspended meteors hoist half region high fell distinctly at last upon himself and family. ⁋ His feasts were none of the liberallest, and far from magnificence, even those two he gave the French Ambassador and the Parliament in 1656, upon their gratulation of his **Syndercombe**[40] deliverance; which last amounted not to above £1000 and she saved £200 of it in the Banquet. For a Big Bellied Woman, a spectator near Cromwell's table, upon the serving thereof with sweetmeats, desiring a few dry candies of apricots, **Colonel Pride**[41] sitting at the same, instantly threw into her apron a conserve of wet, with both his hands, and stained it all over; when, as if that had been the sign, Oliver catches up his napkin and throws it at Pride, he at him again, while all of that table were engaged in the scuffle; the noise whereof made the members rise before the sweet-meats were set down, and believing dinner was done, go to this pastime of gambols and be spectators of his Highness's frolics. Were it worth a description, I could give the reader a just and particular account of that *Ahab festival* as it was solemnized in the Banqueting House of Whitehall. ⁋ But I must pass it, and those other nuptial entertainments at the marriage of his daughters, and the treats he gave to **Duke de Crequi**[42] and **Monsieur Mancin**[43] the Cardinal's great counsellors, and Familiar's

---

earnest: foretaste; *Ahab festival:* Ahab was a corrupt king of Israel (see 1 Kings 16.29) so the reference is to a sort of debauched affair; *arrided:* was pleasing to.

Nephew, as things beyond her sphere, and out her charge and my purpose, and instance the common ordinary diet of this family, whereby the reader will better perceive, and be perhaps advantaged also by the intention and nature of this discourse. ❡ Here follows the most usual meat and diet observed at her table, most of them ordinary and vulgar except some few rarities, but such as *arrided* her palate and expense, of which it will be no unpleasing labour to the reader to peruse the cookery and manner of dressing, as also her preserves etc.

(46)

Here followes the most usual Meat and Diet observed at her Table, most of them ordinary and vulgar, except some few Rarities, but such as arrided her Palate and Expence, of which it will be no unpleasing Labour to the Reader, to peruse the Cookery, and manner of Dressing, as also her Preserves, &c.

Ho

[47]

How to make a Rare Dutch Pudding.

TAke a pound and a half of Fresh Beef, all lean, take a pound and a quarter of Beef Suet, sliced both very small, then take a half penny stale Loaf and grate it, a handful of Sage, and a little Winter Savory, a little Time, shred these very small; take four Eggs, half a pint of Cream, a few Cloves, Nutmegs, Mace and Pepper finely beaten, mingle them altogether very well, with a little Salt, roll it all up together in a green Colwort Leaf, and then tye it up hard in a Linnen Cloth, garnish your Dish with grated bread, and serve it up with Mustard in Sawcers.

E 3

How

Double page spread from the original book in the Cromwell Museum

How to make a
rare Dutch Pudding.

Take a pound and a half of fresh beef, all lean, take a pound and a quarter of beef suet, sliced both very small, then take a half-penny stale loaf and grate it, a handful of sage and a little *Winter savory*, a little thyme, shred these very small; take four eggs, half a pint of cream, a few cloves, nutmegs, mace and pepper finely beaten, mingle them all together very well, with a little salt; roll it all up together in a green *colewort* leaf and then tie it up hard in a linen cloth, garnish your dish with grated bread and serve it up with mustard in saucers.

How to roast a leg of mutton
the French way.

Take half a pound of mutton and quarter of a pound of suet, season it with sweet herbs and a little nutmeg and two or three shallots, slice these very small and stuff the mutton round, then take some of the best *Hackney turnips* and boil them in beef broth very tender, then squeeze the water from them a little, set them in a dish under the leg of mutton when it is half roasted and so let the gravy drop into them, and when the meat is roasted serve them in the dish with it with a little fresh butter and vinegar, garnish your dish with sliced onions and parsley and some of the turnip sliced.

How to make
Scotch *collops* of veal
(this was almost her
constant dish).

Take a fillet of veal, cut it out into very broad slices, fat and lean, not too thick; take eight eggs, beat them very well with a little salt, grate a whole nutmeg, take a handful of thyme and strip it; take a pound of sausages, half a pint of stewing **oysters**[44], the largest to be had, wash and cleanse them from the gravel; then half fry your veal with *sweet butter*, then put in your sausages and oysters; then take a quarter of a pound of *capers*, shred them very small; three anchovies, dissolve them in white wine and fair water, so put in your eggs, shred capers and anchovies, butter and spice, and mingle them, and strew them in the pan upon the veal and oysters; serve it with *sippets*, with a little fresh butter, vinegar and lemons sliced, and *barberries*, with a little salt. You must have a care to keep the meat stirring, lest the eggs curdle with the heat of the fire.

How to souse a pig and collar it like a Brawn.

After you have stuck the pig let him bleed well, then with scalding water and *Rozin* finely beaten take off the hair. Let him lie in cold water a little space, shifted two or three times, that he may look white, then cut off the feet, slit him open and take out his inwards and cut off his head. Take the two sides asunder, lay them in cold water, steep it there a day and a night, shifting the water thrice. Then take out the bones, roll up each side several, tying them as hard as possible in the fashion of a collar of brawn, then tie it up in a cloth hard and put the head whole in another. Then boil it in water and salt, cloves, mace and nutmeg and a handful of rosemary and some sweet herbs *while* it is very tender; take it up and let it cool, then put it into the liquor that boiled it, adding thereto two quarts of *small beer;* set the two collars in a dish garnished with salt (with the head entire in the middle) and stick in two sprigs of rosemary in flower and serve it with saucers of mustard.

How to make a sweet pie with *lambstones* and sweetbreads and sugar.

Take the *lambstones* and slit them in the middle and skin them. Wash the sweetbreads both of veal and lamb and wipe them very dry; take the lamb's liver and shred it very small; take the udder of a leg of veal and slice with it. Season all with a little salt, nutmeg, mace and cloves beaten, and two whole pepper. Then shred two or three *pippins* and candied lemon and orange peel, half a dozen dates sliced, with currants and white sugar, a few caraway seeds, a quarter of a pint of *verjuice* and as much rosewater; a couple of eggs. Roll up all these together in little puddings or balls made green with the juice of spinach, and lay a pudding, then a sweetbread and then a lambstone till you have filled up the pie, and cover them with dates and sliced *citron* and lemon. When it is *drawn* take two or three yolks of eggs, beat them and put them to a little fresh butter, white wine and sugar and pour it into the *tunnel*, scrape some loaf sugar upon the lid and so serve it.

A rare White-pot.

Take three pints of cream, *whole cinnamon*, a little *sliced* nutmeg, set on the cream and spice and scald it. Take a penny loaf, slice it very thin. Take a couple of marrow bones, lay the marrow sliced on the bottom of the dish, upon the marrow lay the bread, then lay *Raisins of the Sun* over the bread, and lay marrow again as before. To the 3 pints of scalded cream add 9 yolks of eggs well beaten with rosewater, sweeten the cream with white sugar and take out the whole cinnamon, and beat the cream and eggs well. Fill up a broad shallow basin and bake it; when 'tis enough scrape fine sugar on it and stick it with red and white *muscadoes*, and so serve it.

A rare *Citron* Pudding.

Take a penny loaf and grate it, a pint and a half of cream, half a dozen of eggs, one nutmeg sliced, a little salt, an ounce of candied citron sliced small, a little candied orange peel sliced, 3 ounces of sugar. Put those into a wooden dish well floured and covered with a cloth, and when the water boileth put it in; boil it well, and serve it up with rosewater and sugar and stick it with wafers or blanched almonds.

How to make Liver Puddings.

Take the guts of a young hog, wash them very clean and lay them two or three days in the water. Take the liver of the same hog and boil it till it will grate, then grate it very small and fine, take to the weight of the liver almost the weight of beef suet, season it with salt, cloves, mace and nutmeg, finely beaten, a penny loaf grated, a pound of the best white sugar, two pound of good currants, a pint of good cream, a quarter of a pint of rose-water, three eggs. Mix all together to such a thickness as you may fill the guts, then prick them and put them into boiling water, and keep an even fire for half a quarter of an hour, then take them up and lay them upon straw; you must have a care in boiling them that you tie them not too hard nor too slack, lest they break.

How to make Marrow Pudding (which she usually had to her breakfast).

Take a pound of the best Jordan almonds, blanch them, beat them fine in a stone or wooden mortar (not in brass) with a little rose-water, take a pound of fine powder sugar, a penny loaf grated; grated nutmeg, a pint of cream, the marrow of two marrow-bones, two *grains* of *ambergris;* mingle them all together with a little salt, fill the skins, boil them gently as before.

How to make Marrow Pasties.

Take some marrow and apples, shred the marrow and apples and put to them a little sugar; put them into puff pastry and fry them in a pan with fresh butter and serve them up to the table with a little white sugar strowed in it.

A country way to make Sausages.

Take pork, not so much fat as lean, mince it exceeding small together, then take part of the *fleck* of pork, which is the suet, in pieces about the bigness of the top of your finger, season each apart with minced sage, good store of pepper and salt, some cloves and mace; mix in the

seasoning into each of them; take the small
sheep's guts and cleanse them (others use
capon's guts) and fill them with your funnel,
always putting some of the fleck between the
minced. If you have it ready you may sprinkle a
little *sack* on the top of the sausage meat, it will
make it fill the better.

Another way [to make sausages].

Cut a gammon that is very red and half boil it,
mince it very small. If the gammon be not fat
take half as much lard of bacon, mince it
likewise, mingle them together and beat them in
a mortar. Season it with thyme and sage minced
very small, and good store of pepper, beaten to
dust, with a little cloves, mace and netmeg, and
a pretty quantity of salt, for they must taste of
that very strong. Add to them the yolk of two
eggs, and so much red wine as will bring them
up into a stiff body, mingle them well with your
hands, fill them into middle skins as big as
ordinary sausages, then hang them in the
chimney for a time. They are not to be eaten in
the skin, but must be cut out very thin
roundways, and do serve for salad all the year
long.

To make green sauce.

Take a handful, or a greater quantity of *sorrel*,
beat it in a mortar with *pippins* pared and
quartered, add thereto a little vinegar and
sugar, put it into saucers. Otherwise take sorrel,
beat it and stamp it well in a mortar, squeeze
out the juice of it, put thereto a little vinegar,
sugar and two hard eggs minced small, a little
butter and grated nutmeg, set this upon the
coals till it is hot, and pour it into the dish on the
sippets. This is sauce for hen or veal and bacon.

To dress udders and tongues.

When they are boiled enough in the beef pot and
skinned, you must have your turnips ready
boiled, cut in pieces and soaked in butter, or
otherwise cauliflowers and carrots, or all of

them; then put the turnips all over the bottom of a large dish, then slice out the tongues and lay the sides one against another, slice the udders and lay them between, opposite to one another, garnish the cauliflowers all over them and the carrots up and down between the cauliflowers, with barberries and parsley in the brim of the dish.

To make gooseberry creams.

First boil, or you may preserve your gooseberries, then having a clear cream boiled up and seasoned with old cinnamon, nutmeg, mace, sugar, rosewater and eggs, dish it up and when it is cold take up the gooseberries with a pin and stick them on in rounds as thick as they can lie upon the said cream, garnishing your dish with them, and strow them over with the finest sugar and serve them up.

To make *Punnado*.

Take one quart of running water put it on the fire in a *skillet*, then cut a light roll of bread in slices about the bigness of a *groat* and as thin as wafers, lay it on a dish on a few coals, then put it into the water with two handfuls of currants, picked and washed, a little large mace, season it with sugar and rosewater when it is enough.

To make a *sack* posset.

Set a gallon of milk on the fire, put therein whole cinnamon and large mace, when it boils stir in a half or whole pound of *Naples biscuit* grated very small, keeping of it stirring while it boils, then beat 8 eggs together, casting of the white away, beat them well with a ladleful of milk, then take the milk off the fire and stir in the eggs, then put it on again, but keep it stirring for fear of curdling, then make ready a pint of sack, warming it upon coals with a little rose-water; season your milk with sugar and pour it into the sack in a large basin and stir it apace, then strow on a good deal of beaten cinnamon and so serve it up.

To make a made dish of apples.

Put on a *skillet* of water with some currants
a-boiling; then pare about a dozen of *pippins*
and cut them from the core into the said water,
when they are boiled tender pour them into a
colander, when the water is drained from them
put them into a dish and season them (but if you
have time stay until they are cold lest it melt
your sugar, besides it will spoil the taste) with
sugar, rosewater, cinnamon and caraway seeds,
then roll out two sheets of pastry. Put one in the
dish bottom and all over the brims, then lay in
the apples in the bottom round and high, wet it
round and cover it with the other sheet; close it
and carve it about the brims of the dish as you
please, prick it and bake it, scrape sugar upon it
and serve it up.

To roast eels.

When they are *flayed*, cut them to pieces about
three or four inches long, dry them and put
them into a dish, mince a little Thyme, two
onions, a piece of lemon peel, a little pepper
beaten small, nutmeg, mace and salt. When it is
cut exceeding small, strow it on the eels with the
yolk of two or three eggs, then having a small
spit (otherwise a couple of square sticks made
for that purpose) split through the eels cross
ways and put a bayleaf between every piece of
eel; and tying the sticks on a spit let them roast.
You need not turn them constantly but let them
stand until they hiss or are brown, so do them
on the other side, and put the dish (in which the
eel was with the seasoning) underneath to save
the gravy, baste it over with *sweet butter*. The
sauce must be a little claret wine, some minced
oysters with their liquor, a grated nutmeg and
an onion with some *sweet butter*, and so serve it.

To make an eel pie.

Your eels being *flayed*, washed and cut in pieces
as long as you think convenient, put to them a
handful of sweet herbs, parsley minced with an
onion, season them with pepper, salt, cloves,
mace and nutmeg, and having your *coffin* made
of good pastry put them in and strew over them

two handfuls of currants and a lemon cut in slices, then put on butter and close the pie. When it is baked put in at the funnel a little *sweet butter,* white wine and vinegar beaten up with a couple of yolks of eggs.

To dress a cod's head.

Cut off the cod's head beyond the gills, that you may have part of the body with it, boil it in water and salt to which you may add half a pint of vinegar, the head must be little more than covered before you put it into the cauldron. Take a quart of the biggest cleanest **oysters**[(44)] and a bunch of sweet herbs and onions, and put them into the mouth of the head, and with a pack-thread bind the jaws fast. You must be sure to pick it and wash it very clean. When it is boiled enough, take it up and set it a-drying over a *chafing-dish* of coals, then take the oyster liquor, four anchovies and a sliced onion; put to them a quarter of a pint of white wine and sweet butter and melt them together, and pour it on the cod's head. Stick all or most of the oysters upon the head, or where they will enter, and garnish it over with them, grate on a little nutmeg and *send it smoking up,* garnish the brims of the dish with lemon and sliced bay leaves.

To boil Perches.

Let your liquor boil, and your pan be seasoned with a little white wine, a couple of onions cut in halves and a bunch of sweet herbs and a little white pepper. Boil them up very quick and *flay* them on both sides, and dish them upon *sippets,* then take a little white wine, gravy, and vinegar, with a grated nutmeg, and almost boil it over a *chafing-dish,* then pour *sweet butter* over it; garnish it with *barberries* and sliced lemons.

To boil eels.

Cut the eels as before and stew them. When they are half done beat a little ale with vinegar and put into the liquor, with some parsley and sweet herbs. Dish them and serve them up in their broth with a little salt.

To boil Woodcocks or Snipes.

Boil them either in strong broth or in water and salt, and being boiled take out the guts and chop them small with the liver, put to it some crumbs of grated white bread, a little of the broth of the cock and some large mace; stew them together with some gravy, then dissolve the yolks of two eggs with some wine vinegar and a little grated nutmeg, and when you are ready to dish it put the eggs to it, and stir it amongst the sauce with a little butter; dish them on *sippets* and run the sauce over them with some beaten butter and capers, or lemon minced small, *barberries* or whole pickled grapes. Sometimes with this sauce boil some sliced onions, and currants boiled in a broth by itself; when you boil it with onions rub the bottom of the dish with garlic.

How to boil *Cocks**
or Larks other ways.

Boil them with the guts in them in strong broth, or fair water, and three or four whole onions, large mace and salt. The cocks being boiled, make sauce with some thin slices of *manchet* or grated bread in another *pipkin* and some of the broth where the fowl or the cocks boil, then put to it some butter and the guts and liver minced, then have some yolks of eggs dissolved with some vinegar, and some grated nutmeg, put it to the other ingredients, stir them together and dish the fowl on fine *sippets*, pour on the sauce with some sliced lemon, grapes or *barberries*, and run it over with beaten butter.

To boil Capons, Pullets,
Chickens, Pigeons, Pheasants
or Partridges.

Fearce them either with the bone or boned, then take off the skin whole, with the legs, wings,

* Woodcocks in this recipe,

neck and head on. Mince the body with some bacon or beef-suet, season it with nutmeg, pepper, cloves, *beaten ginger*, salt and a few sweet herbs finely minced and mingled among some 3 or 4 yolks of eggs, some sugar, whole grapes, gooseberries, *barberries* and *pistaches;* fill the skins and *prick* them up in the back, then stew them between two dishes with some strong broth, white wine, butter, some large mace, marrow, gooseberries and sweet herbs; being stewed serve them on *sippets* with some marrow and sliced lemon; in winter, currants.

To boil a Chicken or Capon in white broth.

First boil the capon in water and salt, then take three pints of strong broth and quart of white wine, and stew it in a *pipkin* with a quarter of a pound of dates, half a pound of fine sugar, four or five blades of large mace, the marrow of 3 marrow bones, a handful of white endive; stew these in a *pipkin* very leisurely, that it may but only simmer, then being finely stewed and the broth well tasted, strain the yolks of ten eggs with some of the broth. Before you dish up the capons or chickens, put in the eggs into the broth, and keep it stirring that it may not curdle, give it a *walm* and set it from the fire. The fowls being dished up, put on the broth, and garnish the meat with dates, marrow, large mace, endive, preserved *barberries* and oranges, boiled *skirrets*, pomegranates and kernels. Make a *lear* of almond paste and grape *verjuice*.

A Turkish dish of meat.

Take an *interlarded* piece of beef, cut it into thin slices and put it into a pot that hath a close cover, or stewing pan, then put into it a good quantity of clean picked rice, skin it very well and put into it a quantity of whole pepper, two or three whole onions, and let this boil very well, then take out the onions and dish it on *sippets*, the thicker it is the better.

To stew a fillet
of beef in the Italian fashion.

Take a young tender fillet of beef and take away
all the skins and sinews clean from it, put to it
some good white wine (that is not too sweet) in a
bowl, wash it and crush it well in the wine, then
strow upon it a little pepper and a powder called
"Tamara" in Italian, and as much salt as will
season it, mingle them very well and put to it as
much white wine as will cover it, lay a *trencher*
upon it to keep it down in a close pan with a
weight on it, and let it steep two nights and a
day; then take it out and put it into a *pipkin*
with some good beef broth, but put none of the
pickle to it, but only beef broth, and that sweet,
not salt; cover it close and set it on the embers,
then put to it a few whole cloves and mace; and
let it stew till it be enough, it will be very tender
and of an excellent taste; serve it with the same
broth as much as will cover it. ℂ To make this
"Tamara", take two ounces of coriander seed,
an ounce of aniseed, an ounce of fennel seed,
two ounces of cloves, and an ounce of cinnamon; beat them into a *gross* powder, with a
little powder of *winter savory*, and put them
into a *vial* glass to keep.

To make an excellent pottage
called Skinke.

Take a leg of beef and chop it into three pieces,
then boil it in a pot with three *pottles* of spring
water, a few cloves, mace and whole pepper;
after the pot is skimmed, put in a bundle of
sweet marjoram, rosemary, thyme, *winter savory*, sage and parsley bound up hard, some salt
and two or three great onions whole; then about
an hour before dinner put in three marrow-
bones, and thicken it with some strained
oatmeal, or *manchet* sliced and steeped with
some gravy, strong broth or some of the
pottage; then a little before you dish up the
skinke, put into it a little fine powder of saffron,
and give it a *walm* or two; dish it on large slices
of French bread, and dish the marrow bones on
them in a fine clean large dish; then have two or
three manchets cut into toasts, and being finely

toasted, lay on the knuckle of beef in the middle
of the dish, the marrow bones round about it,
and the toasts round about the dish brim. Serve
it hot.

To stew a Rump, or the fat end of a Brisket of Beef in the French fashion.

Take a rump of beef, boil it and skim it clean in
a stewing pan or broad mouthed *pipkin*, cover it
close and let it stew an hour; then put to it some
whole pepper, cloves, mace and salt, *scotch* the
meat with your knife to let out the gravy, then
put in some claret wine and half a dozen sliced
onions; having boiled, an hour after put in some
capers, or a handful of *broom buds*, and half a
dozen of cabbage-lettuce being first parboiled
in fair water and quartered, two or three
spoonfuls of wine vinegar and as much *verjuice*,
and let it stew till it be tender; then serve it on
sippets of French bread and dish it on those
sippets; blow off the fat clean off the broth, or
skim it, and stick it with fried bread.

To boil a Chine, Rump, Sirloin, Brisket, Rib, Flank, Buttock, or Fillet of Beef *powdered*.

Take any of these and give them in summer a
week's *powdering*, in winter a fortnight. Stuff
them or plain; if you stuff them do it with all
manner of sweet herbs, fat beef minced and
some nutmeg. Serve them on *brewis*, with roots
or cabbage boiled in milk, with beaten butter
etc.

To pickle roast beef, Chine, Sirloin, Rib, Brisket, Flank or *Neat's Tongues*.

Take any of the aforesaid beef, as chine or
fore-rib, and stuff it with *pennyroyal* or other
sweet herbs, or parsley minced small, and some
salt, prick in here and there a few whole cloves,
and roast it; then take claret wine, wine vinegar,

whole pepper, rosemary, and bay, and thyme bound up close in a bundle and boiled in some claret wine and wine vinegar, make the pickle and put some salt to it, then pack it up close in a barrel that will but just hold it, put the pickle to it, close it on the head and keep it for your use.

To stew Beef in gobbets in the French fashion.

Take a flank of beef or any part but the leg, cut it into slices or gobbets as big as a pullet's egg, with some gobbets of fat, and boil it in a pot or *pipkin* with some fair spring water. Skim it clean and put to it an hour after it hath boiled, carrots, parsnips, turnips, great onions, salt, some cloves, mace, and whole pepper, cover it close and stew it till it be very tender; then half an hour before dinner put into it some picked thyme, parsley, *winter savory*, sweet marjoram, sorrel and spinach (being a little bruised with the back of a ladle) and some claret wine; then dish it on fine *sippets* and serve it to the table hot, garnish it with grapes, *barberries* or gooseberries. Sometimes use spices, the bottoms of boiled artichokes put into beaten butter and grated nutmeg, garnished with barberries.

Stewed *collops* of Beef.

Take of the buttock of beef thin slices, cross the grain of the meat, then hack them and fry them in *sweet butter*, and being fried fine and brown, put them in a *pipkin* with some strong broth, a little claret wine, and some nutmeg, stew it very tender; and half an hour before you dish it put to it some good gravy, *elder vinegar*, and a clove or two; when you serve it put some juice of orange and three or four slices on it, stew down the gravy somewhat thick, and put into it when you dish it some beaten butter.

Olives of Beef stewed and roast.

Take a buttock of beef and cut some of it into thin slices as broad as your hand, then hack them with the back of the knife, lard with small lard and season them with pepper, salt and nutmeg; then make a *farcing* with some sweet herbs, thyme, onions, the yolks of hard eggs, beef suet or lard all minced, some salt, *barberries*, grapes or gooseberries; season it with the former spices lightly, and work it up together, then lay it on the slices and roll them up round with some *caul* of veal, beef or mutton, bake them in a dish in the oven or roast them, then put them in a pipkin with some butter and saffron, or none, blow off the fat from the gravy and put it to them, with some artichokes, potato, or *skirrets* blanched, being first boiled, a little claret wine, and serve them on *sippets* with some sliced orange, lemon, *barberries*, grapes or gooseberries.

To boil a Capon or Chicken with cauliflowers.

Cut off the buds of your flowers and boil them in milk with a little mace till they be very tender, then take the yolks of 2 eggs and strain them with a quarter of a pint of *sack*, then take as much thick butter being drawn* with a little vinegar and a sliced lemon, brew them together; then take the flowers out of the milk, put them to the butter and sack, dish up your capon being tender boiled upon *sippets* finely carved, and pour on the sauce, serve it to the table with a little salt.

To boil a Capon or Chicken with Asparagus.

Boil your capon or chicken in fair water and some salt, then put in their bellies a little mace, chopped parsley and *sweet butter;* being boiled, serve them on *sippets* and put a little of the broth on them; then have a bundle or two of asparagus boiled, put in beaten butter and serve it on your capon or chicken.

* See recipe for "Drawn butter" on p.[77 MS].

A rare Fricassee.

Take six pigeons and six chicken *peepers*, scald and truss them being drawn clean, head and all on, then set them and have some *lamb-stones* and sweetbreads blanched, parboiled and sliced, fry most of the sweetbreads floured, have also some asparagus ready, cut off the tops an inch long, the yolks of two hard eggs, pistachios, the marrow of six marrow bones, half the marrow *fried green*, and white batter. Let it be kept warm till it be almost dinner time, then have a clean frying pan and fry the fowl with good *sweet butter*, being finely fried put out the butter and put to them some roast mutton gravy, some large fried oysters and some salt; then put in the hard yolks of eggs and the rest of the sweetbreads that are not fried, the pistachios, asparagus and half the marrow; then stew them well in the frying-pan with some grated nutmeg, pepper (a clove or two of garlic if you please), a little white wine, and let them be well stewed. Then have ten yolks of eggs dissolved in a dish with grape-*verjuice* or wine vinegar, and a little beaten mace and put it to the fricassee, then have a French six-penny loaf sliced into a fair large dish set on coals, with some good mutton gravy, then give the fricassee two or three *walms* on the fire, and pour it on the *sops* in the dish; garnish it with fried sweetbread, fried oysters, fried marrow, pistachios, sliced almonds, and the juice of two or three oranges.

To boil a Capon,
Pullet, or Chicken.

Boil them in good mutton broth, with mace, a faggot of sweet herbs, sage, spinach, marigold leaves and flowers, white or green endive, *borage*, *bugloss*, parsley and *sorrel*, and serve it on *sippets*.

To boil Capons or Chickens
with sage and parsley.

First boil them in water and salt, then boil some parsley, sage, two or three eggs hard, chop them, then have a few thin slices of fine *manchet* and stew all together, but break not the slices of bread; stew them with some of the broth wherein the chickens boil, some large mace, butter, a little white wine or vinegar, with a few *barberries* or grapes; dish up the chickens on the sauce and run them over with *sweet butter* and lemon cut like dice, the peel cut like small lard, and boil a little peel with the chickens.

To boil a Capon or Chicken with diverse compositions.

Take off the skin whole but leave on the legs, wings and heads, mince the body with some beef-suet or lard, put to it some sweet herbs minced and season it with cloves, mace, pepper, salt, two or three eggs, grapes, gooseberries or *barberries*, bits of potato or mushrooms; in the winter with sugar, currants and prunes. Fill the skin, prick it up and stew it between two dishes with large mace and strong broth, pieces of artichokes, *cardoons* or asparagus and marrow; being finely stewed, serve it on carved *sippets* and run it over with beaten butter, lemon sliced, and scrape on sugar.

To boil a Capon, Chicken with *Cardoons*, Mushrooms, Artichokes or Oysters.

The aforesaid fowls being parboiled and cleansed from the grounds, stew them finely; then take your *cardoons* being cleansed and peeled into water, have a *skillet* of fair water boiling hot, and put them therein; being tender boiled, take them up and fry them in chopped lard or *sweet butter*, pour away the butter and put them into a *pipkin*, with strong broth, pepper, mace, ginger, *verjuice* and the juice of [an] orange; stew all together with some *strained* almonds and some sweet herbs chopped, give them a *walm*, and serve your capon or chicken on *sippets*. Let them be *searsed* and wrap your *searst* fowl in *cauls* of veal, half roast them, then stew them in a pipkin with the aforesaid cardoons and broth.

To boil any land fowl, as, Turkey, *Bustard*, Pheasant, Peacock, Partridge, or the like.

Take a turkey and flay off the skin, leave the legs and rumps whole, then mince the flesh raw with some beef-suet or lard, season it with some nutmeg, pepper, salt, and some minced sweet herbs, then put to it some yolks of raw eggs, mingle all together with 2 bottoms of boiled artichokes, roasted chestnuts blanched, some marrow, and some boiled *skirrets* or parsnips cut like dice, or some pleasant pears, and yolks of hard eggs in quarters, some gooseberries, grapes or *barberries;* fill the skin and *prick it up* in the back; stew it in a stewing pan or deep dish and cover it with another; but first put some strong broth to it, some marrow, artichokes boiled and quartered, large mace, white wine, chestnuts, quarters of pears, salt, grapes, barberries and some of the meat made up in balls stewed, serve it on fine carved *sippets*, broth it, and lay on the garnish with slices of lemon and whole lemon-peel, run it over with beaten butter and garnish the dish with chestnuts, yolks of hard eggs, and large mace. ¶ For the *lears* or thickening, yolks of hard eggs strained with some of the broth, or strained almond paste with some of the broth, or else strained bread and *sorrel.* ¶ Otherwise you may boil the former fowls either boned and trussed up with a *farcing* of some minced veal or mutton, and seasoned as the former in all points with those materials, or boil it with the bones in, being trussed up. A turkey to bake, and break the bones. ¶ Otherwise bone the fowl, and fill the body with the aforesaid farcing, or make a pudding of grated bread, minced suet of beef or veal, seasoned with cloves, mace, pepper, salt and grapes, fill the body and prick it up the back and stew it as aforesaid. ¶ Or make the pudding of grated bread, beef suet minced, some currants, nutmegs, cloves, sugar, sweet herbs, salt, juice of spinach; if yellow, saffron, some minced meat, cream, eggs and barberries; fill the fowl and stew it in mutton broth and white wine, with the gizzard, liver and bones, stew it down well, then have some artichoke bottoms boiled and quartered, some potatoes boiled and blanched, and some dates quartered, also some marrow boiled in water and salt; for the garnish some boiled skirret or pleasant pears. Then make a lear of almond paste strained with mutton broth for the thickening of the former broth. ⁋ Otherwise simply being stuffed with parsley, serve it with butter, vinegar and parsley boiled and minced; as also bacon boiled on it or about it, in two pieces, and two saucers of green sauce. ⁋ Or otherwise for variety boil your fowl in water and salt, then take strong broth and put in a faggot of sweet herbs, mace, marrow, cucumber sliced, and thin slices of *interlarded* bacon, and salt, etc.

To boil Capon or Chicken with *sugar peas*.

When the *cods* be but young, string them and pick off the husk; then take two or three handfuls and put them into a *pipkin* with half a pound of *sweet butter*, a quarter of a pint of fair water, *gross* pepper, salt, mace and some salad oil; stew them till they be very tender, and strain to them 3 or 4 yolks of eggs with six spoonfuls of *sack*.

To make a *Neat's*-Tongue Pie.

Take a couple of neat's tongues and almost boil them, then cut out the meat at the butt end as far as you can, not breaking it out at the sides, put a little suet to the said meat you cut out, a few sweet herbs and parsley mingled all together very small, season it with a little pepper, salt, cloves, mace, ginger, and a handful of grated bread, a little sugar and the yolks of three or four eggs, mould it up into a body, season your tongues in the inside and outside with your seasoning aforesaid and wash them within with the yolk of an egg, and force them where you cut forth the meat, and make a forcemeat of the residues; then having the *coffin* made in the form of a neat's tongue, lay them in with the puddings little balls to them, put in dates and shred lemon with butter on the top and close it up; when it is baked, put in a *lear* of the Venison Sauce, which is claret wine, a handful of grated bread, cinnamon, ginger, sugar and a little vinegar, boil them up so thick as it may only run like butter, it ought to be sharp and sweet; this sauce serves for any part of venison, washed the shoulders, sides and haunches, which if seasoned must be laid in water, and when roasted must be served up stuck with rosemary.

To roast a Leveret or Hare.

Case your leveret, but cut not off their hinder legs nor ears, but hack one leg through another, so likewise cut a hole through one ear and put it through the other; in the meantime make your sauce with a little thyme, sweet marjoram and *winter savory* very small, with the liver of the hare boiled and the yolks of three or four hard eggs, with a little bacon and beef suet. Boil this well up with water and vinegar, when it is boiled add a grated nutmeg, *sweet butter* and a little sugar and dish your hare; the same may you make to rabbits.

To stew Ducks the French Fashion.

Take the duck and half roast it, put half a score onions in the belly whole, some whole pepper, a bundle of thyme, a little salt, when it is half roasted take it up and slash it into pieces, put it between two dishes and *pierce the gravy*, mix some claret wine with that gravy and a little sliced nutmeg, a couple of anchovies, wash them and slit them, slice the onions in the duck's belly, cover the dishes close, so let them stew while enough; take some butter, beat it thick and shred a lemon in it and serve it, garnish your dish with lemon peel and your onions.

To make a Pigeon pie.

Truss your pigeons to bake, and set them, and lard the one half of them with bacon. Mince a

few sweet herbs and parsley with a little beef
suet, the yolks of hard eggs and an onion or two,
season it with salt, beaten pepper, cloves, mace
and nutmeg, work it up with a piece of butter
and stuff the bellies of the pigeons, season them
with some salt, beaten pepper, cloves, mace and
beaten nutmeg, take also as many *lambstones*,
seasoned as aforesaid, with six *collops* of bacon
(the salt drawn out). Then make a round *coffin*
and put in your pigeons, and if you will put in
lambstones and sweetbreads and some artichoke bottoms, or other dry meat to soak up the
juice, because the pie will be very sweet and full
of it. Then put a little white wine beaten up with
the yolk of an egg when it comes out of the oven,
and so serve it.

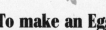

To boil Pigeons
after the Dutch way.

Take your pigeons, set and lard them, put them
into a *pipkin* with so much strong broth (made
of knuckles of veal, and mutton, and beef) and
well cover them. When they are skimmed, put
to them a faggot of sweet herbs, some large
mace, a handful of capers, and *raisins of the
sun* shred very small, six quartered dates, a
piece of butter with three yolks of hard eggs
minced, with a handful of grapes or *barberries*,
then beat two yolks of your eggs with *verjuice*
and some white bread, a ladle of *sweet butter*
and a grated nutmeg; so serve it with *sippets;*
though the modern way is to boil it with *collops*
of bacon and dish it with rice boiled, carrots and
turnips minced small and cauliflowers.

To make an Egg Pie,
or Mince Pie of Eggs.

Take the yolks of two dozen of eggs, shred them,
take the same weight of beef suet, about a
pound, half a dozen *pippins*, a pound of
currants well washed and dried, half a pound of
sugar, a pennyworth of beaten spice, a few
caraway seeds, candied orange peel shred, a
little *verjuice*, some rose-water, fill the *coffin*
and bake it with a gentle heat.

To make a Salad of a cold Hen or Pullet.

Take a hen and roast it, let it be cold, carve up the legs, take the flesh and mince it small, shred a lemon, a little parsley and onions, an apple, a little pepper and salt with oil and vinegar, garnish the dish with the bones and lemon peel and so serve it.

To make a Hash of Capon or Pullet.

Take a capon or partridge and roast them, and being cold mince them very fine, the brains and wings, and tear the legs and rumps whole to be *carbonadoed*, then put some strong mutton broth or good gravy, grated nutmeg, a great onion and salt, then stew them in a large earthen *pipkin* or saucepan. Stew the rumps and legs in the same strong broth in another pipkin, then take some light French bread, chipped, and cover the bottom of the dish, steep the bread in the same broth, or good mutton gravy, then pour the hash on the steeped bread. Lay the legs and the rump on the hash, with some fried oysters, sliced lemon and lemon peel, the juice of an orange, and yolks of eggs strained, and beaten butter. Garnish the dish with carved oranges, lemons etc. Thus you may hash any kind of fowl; there are other whimsical ingredients in the practice of cookery, but I mention only such as have a ready and natural, not forced or foreign relish, which was little used here.

To butter Eggs upon Toasts.

Take twenty eggs, beat them in a dish with some salt and put butter to them, then have two large rolls or fine *manchets*, cut them in toasts and toast them against the fire with a pound of fine *sweet butter*, being finely buttered in a fair clean dish; put the eggs on the toasts and garnish your dish with pepper and salt. Otherwise half boil them in the shells, then butter

them and serve them on toasts or toasts about
them.

To stew a Loin, Leg, Breast of Mutton.

Take a loin of mutton and joint it well, and do so
to the breast, and draw and stuff it with sweet
herbs and minced parsley, then put it in a deep
stewing dish with the right side downwards, put
to it so much white wine and strong broth as will
stew it, set it on a great heap of coals, put in two
or three onions, a bundle of sweet herbs and a
little large mace, when it is almost stewed take a
handful of spinach, parsley and endive and put
into it, at the last you may put some gooseberries or grapes; in the winter-time *samphire*
and *capers*, here you may add them at any time.
Dish up the loin of mutton and put by the liquor
you do not use, and thicken the other with yolks
of eggs and sweet butter, so put on the sauce
and the herbs over the meat and garnish the
dish with lemon and *barberries.*

To hash a Rabbit.

You must take the flesh from the bones of the
rabbit, being before washed, and mince it small
with your mincing knife, so put to it a little
strong broth and vinegar, an onion or two, with
a grated nutmeg and let it stew up together,
then mince a handful of boiled parsley green,
with a lemon cut like dice and a few *barberries,*
put it into the hash and toast it all together, and
when it is enough, put a ladleful of *sweet butter*
to it and dish it upon the *lines,* so garnish it with
lemon.

To Carbonade Mutton.

Boil a shoulder or breast of mutton, then score
them with your knife and strew on minced
thyme and salt and a little nutmeg. When they
are boiled, dish them up; the sauce is claret wine
boiled up with two onions, a little *samphire* and
capers, and a little gravy, garnished with
lemons.

To pickle Oysters.

Take a quart of the largest great oysters, with the liquor, wash them clean and wipe them, add to them a pint of fair water, with half a pint of white wine vinegar, half an ounce of whole pepper, a handful of salt, a quarter of an ounce of large mace, with the liquor of the oysters strained. Put all together in a *pipkin* over a soft fire, let them simmer together a quarter of an hour. When the oysters are enough, take them up and put them into a little fair water and vinegar until they be cold, the pickle boiling a quarter of an hour after the oysters are taken up, both being cold put them up together; when you use them garnish the dish with *barberries* and lemon and a little of the mace and pepper, and pour in some of the pickle.

A way to fry Rabbits
with sweet sauce.

Cut your rabbit in pieces, wash it and dry it well in a cloth, take some fresh butter and fry the rabbit in it, when your rabbit is little more than half fried, take some slices shred very small, a quarter of a pint of cream, the yolks of a couple of eggs, some grated nutmeg and salt; when the rabbit is enough, put them into the pan and stir them all together, take a little vinegar, fresh butter and sugar, melt it together and so serve it with *sippets*, the dish garnished with flowers etc.

How to roast a
rabbit with oysters.

Wash your rabbit and dry it well, take half a pint of oysters, wash them and wipe them clean one by one, and put them into the rabbit's belly, a couple of onions shred, whole pepper, large mace, two or three sprigs of thyme, sew up the belly; for the sauce, as usual, the liver and parsley, a hard egg, shred them together and beat some butter thick, put it into the dish and serve it.

To make a fricassee of chickens.

Take three or four chickens, scald them, *flay* off the skin and feathers together, put them in a little water, take half a pint of white wine and two or three whole onions, some large mace and nutmeg tied up in a cloth, a bundle of sweet herbs and a little salt, and put them all in a *pipkin* closely covered. Let them simmer a quarter of an hour, then take half a dozen yolks of eggs, half a pound of *sweet butter*, four anchovies dissolved in a little of the broth, shred your boiled spice small, take a quarter of a pound of *capers*, shred them very small, put the anchovies dissolved into the eggs and butter and capers, and so stir it all together over a *chafing-dish* of coals till it begins to thicken, then take the chicken[s] out of the broth and pour *lear* upon them, serve them with *sippets* and lemon sliced.

Another way to fry the same fricassee brown.

Take four chickens, scald them and cut them in quarters, beat them flat with your cleaver, and break their bones, dry them with a cloth very well and flour them all over on the skinny sides. Your pan being hot with clarified butter, put them in with the skinny sides downwards, fry them brown, then turn them, let your *lear* be a little claret wine and gravy, then put your liquor out of your pan, and put in your lear, with pieces of sausages wrung off as long as your thumb, and a pint of **oysters,**[44] two or three onions, with a bundle of sweet herbs, a grated nutmeg and two or three anchovies, let them boil up in the pan, then beat the yolks of four eggs with a little strong broth, take the pan off the fire and put them in, if it turns too thick you may thin it with wine, gravy or strong broth, keep it shaking whilst it's on the fire; then dish up your chickens in *sippets*, and pour on your lear and oysters, with your pieces of sausages by the sides of the dish and garnish it with lemon.

A grand salad.

Take a quarter of a pound of *raisins of the sun*, a quarter of a pound of blanched almonds, a quarter of a pound of *capers*, a quarter of a pound of olives, the like quantity of *samphire*, a quarter of a pound of *pickle cucumbers*, a lemon shred, some pickled french beans, a wax tree set in the middle of the dish, pasted to the dish, lay all their quarters round the dish (you may also mince the flesh of a roasted hen, with sturgeon and shrimps) and garnish the dish with cut beans and turnips in several *figures*.

How to pickle French beans.

Take your beans and string them, boil them tender, then take them off and let them stand till they are cold, put them into the pickle of *beer-vinegar*, pepper and salt, cloves and mace, with a little ginger.

A cordial strengthening Broth.

Take a *red cock*, strip off the feathers with the skin, take a rolling-pin and bruise his bones to shivers, set it over the fire and just cover it with water, put in some salt and watch the skimming and boiling of it, put in a handful of *harts-horn*, a quarter of a pound of *blue currants*, as many stoned *raisins of the sun*, as many prunes, four blades of large mace, a bottom crust of a white loaf, half an ounce of *china-root* sliced, being steeped three hours before in warm water, boil in three or four pieces of **gold**(45), strain it and put in a little fine sugar and juice of an orange and so use it.

Another way.

Take a *cock* or two, cut off their wings and legs, cleanse all the blood out of the inside, parboil them very well, that when they are boiled there may arise no scum, then wash them again in fair water, put them in a pitcher with a pint of Rhenish wine, and as much of your aforesaid strong broth as will cover them, add thereto a few cloves, large mace, shred ginger and nutmeg, a little whole pepper with a small quantity of *china* and an ounce or two of *harts-horn*, put a little salt and stop up your pitcher close that no steam may come forth; you must boil the pitcher in a great pot about six hours, then pour out the broth and strain it into a basin, and squeeze into it the juice of two or three lemons. ⁋ These were the ordinary morning draughts, with *caudles* for variety, of the Protectoress and her Master, and about 11 o'clock, a cup of small ale with a toast and sugar.

How to make Barley-broth

Take barley and put in fair water, give it three *qualms* over the fire, separate the waters and put it into a colander, boil it in a fourth water with a blade of mace and a clove, and when it is boiled away put in some raisins and currants, and when the fruit is boiled enough, take it off and season it with *white*, white rose-water, butter and sugar and a couple of yolks of eggs beaten with it. This was a mess frequently prepared for Oliver.

To make a
pudding of Hog's Liver
another way.

Boil your hog's liver and grate it, put to it more grated bread than liver, with as much fine flour as of either, put twelve eggs to the value of a gallon of this mixture, with about two pound of beef suet minced small, with a pound and a half of currants, half a quarter of a pint of rose-water, a good quantity of cloves and mace, nutmeg, cinnamon and ginger all minced very small, mix all these with sweet milk and cream, let it be no thicker than fritter batter to fill your hog's guts. You may make it with the *maw* fit to be eaten hot at table. In your knitting or tying the guts, you must remember to give them three or four inches scope. In your putting them into the boiling water you must handle them round, to bring the meat equal to all parts of the gut, they will ask about half an hour boiling. The boiling must be sober; if the wind rise in them, you must be ready to prick them or else they will fly and burst in pieces. ⁋ This was **Madam Frances**[46] her delicacy.

How to make an Eel Pie with oysters.

Take the eels, wash them and gut them, and dry them well in a cloth, to four good eels allow a pint of oysters well washed. Season them with pepper, salt and nutmeg and large mace, put half a pound of butter into the pie, as also half a lemon sliced, so bake it. When it is drawn take the yolks of two eggs, a couple of anchovies dissolved in a little white wine, with a quarter of a pound of fresh butter, melt it and mix all together and make a *lear* of it and put it into the pie.

How to roast a shoulder of mutton with oysters.

Your oysters being parboiled, put to them some parsley, thyme and *winter savory* minced small, with the yolks of six eggs hard boiled and minced, a half-penny-loaf of grated bread, three or four yolks of eggs, so mingle all together with your hands. Your shoulder of mutton being spitted, lay it upon the dresser and make holes with a sticking knife, in it (you may cut the holes as wide as you think convenient) put in your oysters with the herbs and ingredients after them, about thirty oysters will be enough; let it roast indifferent long, take the rest of a quart and put them into the deep dish with claret wine, two or three onions in halves, a couple of minced anchovies, put all this under your mutton in the pan, so save your gravy, and when your meat is ready put your sauce upon a heap of coals, put to it the yolk of an egg beaten, a grated nutmeg and *sweet butter*, dish the shoulder of mutton and pour this thick *lear* of oysters all over it, and garnish it with *barberries* and lemons.

How to pickle up cucumbers.

Take young gherkins and wipe them clean, take the seeds of dill and fennel, large mace, beaten pepper and salt, season the *beer vinegar* very well with salt, lay a layer of cucumbers and sprinkle between every row of cucumbers your seeds and seasoning. When the pot is almost full with cucumbers, fill it up to the brim with beer vinegar and keep it close covered. If you like *broom buds* rather, they are to be pickled with water and salt, and shut close as before. But I may add (to **put the carior's nose out of joint**)[47] that onions and water were the chief court sauce, and shall henceforth be exalted and dignified by the name of the Protector's **Hogo.**[48]

How to make a fresh cheese.

I have mentioned before her making of butter, I shall now give you an experiment of her making of fresh cheese. Take some new milk or cream, and a *race of cinnamon*. Scald it, then take it off the fire, sweeten it with fine sugar, then take a spoonful of rennet to two quarts of milk, set it by and keep it close covered, and so let it stand. When the cheese comes, strow a little fine sugar and grated nutmeg, and serve it with *sippets*, *sops* in *sack* or *muscadine;* which at this season of the year was one of the extempore entertainments of this rustical lady.

To roast a Lamb or Kid.

Truss your lamb or kid, pricking the head backwards over the shoulder, laying it down, set it and lard it with bacon and draw it with thyme and a little lemon peel, then make a pudding with a little grated bread, a handful of sweet herbs, a handful of beef suet, put in about a handful of flour, and a little sausage with thyme, made mince meat, season it with cloves, mace, cinnamon, ginger, nutmeg and salt, make it up into a tender body with two or three eggs and a little bran, stuff it into the belly of the lamb and kid, put some sauce of veal or lamb over it, so *prick it up* the belly, roast the lamb and kid and when it is enough, serve it up with venison sauce.

To roast Venison.

This is the same common way with roasting a hog's haslet, and merely devised for to take off by its variety the nauseousness of this meat, which was in abundance at their table, as shall further be manifested. Take the biggest part of the haunch of venison, and cut it in thin *collops*, hack it with your knife, as you do the like to veal, then lard it very thick with a small *larding pin*, then take a handful of parsley and spinach, good store of thyme, a little rosemary, *winter-savory* and sweet marjoram, mince it exceeding small with a little beef suet, so put it in the dish with your venison; put to it some beaten cloves, cinnamon, nutmeg, with a pretty quantity of salt, the yolks of half a dozen of eggs or more, mingle it up all together with your hands, then spit your collops on a small spit or long *broaches* made with sticks, you must spit them so by doubling of them or bringing in the ends, that they may not hang too long, but equal; when they are all spitted, put your herbs amongst them and tie them together with a pack-thread; as they roast put a dish under them with claret wine; when they are almost done, take your dish and set it on the coals, put grated bread, beaten cinnamon, vinegar and sugar to the wine, with a ladleful of drawn butter, dish up your venison and put on this *lear*, but very thin over it, and so serve it.

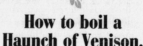

How to boil a Haunch of Venison.

This was a truly Royal and constant dish in its season at court, when it was so really, and therefore out of curiosity and state was served up to her table during the season; it is more extraordinary than any of the former, but since her times destroyed the game yet cheapened and aviled the venison and made it everyone's meat, which sordid example yet prevails among some proprietors of parks, I will set down this direction. ❦ First stuff your venison with a handful of sweet herbs and parsley minced, with a little beef suet and yolks of eggs boiled hard, season your stuffing with pepper, nutmeg, ginger and salt, put your haunch of venison a-boiling, being *powdered* before, then boil up three of four cauliflowers in strong broth and a little milk; when they are boiled, put them forth into a *pipkin*, add to them drawn butter and keep them warm by the fire, then boil up two or three handfuls of spinach in the same liquor, when it is boiled up pour out part of your broth and put in a little vinegar, a ladleful of *sweet butter* and a grated nutmeg; your dish being ready with *sippets* in the bottom, put on the spinach round towards your dish side, then take up the venison being boiled and put it in the middle of your dish and put in your cauliflowers all over it, pour on your sweet butter over your cauliflowers and garnish it with *barberries*, and the brims of the dish with some green parsley minced. Cabbage is as good done in the same manner as cauliflowers.

How to bake a Venison-Pasty.

This is called the King of dainties, which Oliver stole by retail (as he did a more real Regality) many years before, and shared this sovereign delicacy among his accomplices. But now, more than bold Robin Hood, he was lord and avowed master of the game, and therefore that his fellow deer stealers may know how to dress their prey à la mode Cromwellian, take this prescription, for to other persons it will be of no use. When you have *powdered* your haunch of venison, or the sides of it, by taking away all the bones and sinews and the skin or fat, season it with pepper and salt only, beat it with your rolling-pin and proportion it for the pasty by taking away from one part and adding to another. Your paste being made with a *peck* of fine flour and about three pound of butter and a dozen eggs, work it up with cold water into as stiff a paste as you can, *drive it forth* for your pasty, let it be as thick as a man's thumb, roll it up upon a rolling-pin and put under it a couple of sheets of *cap-paper* well floured, then your *white* being already minced and beaten with water, proportion it upon the pasty to the breadth and length of the venison, so lay your venison in the said white, wash it round with your feather and put on a border; season your venison at the top and turn over your other leaf of paste, so close up your pasty, then drive out another border for garnishing the sides up to the top of the pasty, so close it up together by the rolling-pin, by rolling it up and down by the sides and ends; and when you have flourished your garnishing and edged your pasty, vent it at the top, set it into the oven and after four or five hours baking at least, draw it. This will serve, abating the time, for any other meats baking, for beef or mutton, and may be applied, which is the main design of this discovery, to vulgar use. I must omit her manner of collaring of venison, because not practicable among mean people.

To boil any usual joint of meat.

Cut any of them in such large pieces as you usually do a neck of mutton, as that two or three of them may serve in a dish, and put them into a pot with so much water as will cover them; if you have a loin of mutton (the suet taken from it) or a neck of veal, you may take ten sprigs of *winter-savory* and as much of thyme, adding to them twelve great onions, if they are small take the more. Grate to them half a penny loaf, with half an ounce of cloves and mace and one handful of spinach, a little salt and parsley (if in the Spring or Summer, otherwise *capers* and *samphire*). Let it boil moderately until it be half consumed, when you take it off, add a little vinegar and *sweet butter*. But you must not let your spinach and parsley have above a quarter of an hour's boiling.

To bake Steaks the French way.

Season the steaks with pepper, nutmeg and salt lightly, and set them by, then take a piece of the leanest of a leg of mutton and mince it small with some beef suet and a few sweet herbs, as tops of thyme and *penny-royal*, grated bread, yolks of eggs, sweet cream, *raisins of the sun*, etc. Work all these together and make it into little balls or puddings, put them (into a deep round pie) on the steaks, then put to them some butter and sprinkle it with *verjuice*, close it up and bake it. When it is enough, cut it up and liquor it with the juice of two or three oranges or lemons.

To bake a pig.

This is an experiment practised by her at Huntingdon brewhouse, and is a singular and the only way of dressing a pig. Take a good quantity of clay, such as they stop barrels' bungs with, and having moulded it, stick your pig and blood him well; and when he is warm, arm him like a **cuirassier**(49) or one of Cromwell's Ironsides, hair, skin and all (his entrails drawn and belly sewed up again) with this prepared clay, thick everywhere, then throw him below the stoke-hole under the furnace and there let him *soak*, turn him now and then, when the clay is hardened, for twelve hours, he is then sufficiently baked; then take him and break off the clay, which easily parts, and you will have a fine crispy coat and all the juice of the pig in your dish; remember but to put a few leaves of sage and a little salt in the belly of it and you need no other sauce. The like you may do with any fowl whatsoever, for the clay will fetch off and consume the feathers.

Another way according to Court fashion.

Flay a small fat pig, cut it in quarters or in smaller pieces, season it with pepper, ginger and salt, lay it into a fit *coffin*. Strip and mince small a handful of parsley, six sprigs of *winter-savory*, strew it on the meat in the pie and strew upon that the yolks of three or four hard eggs minced, and lay upon them five or six blades of mace, a handful of clusters of *barberries*, a handful of currants well washed and picked, a little sugar, half a pound of *sweet butter* or more. Close your pie and set it in an oven, as hot as for *manchet*, and in three hours it will be baked. Draw it forth and put in half a pint of sugar, being warmed upon the fire, pour it all over the meat and put on the pie lid again, scrape on sugar and serve it hot on the table.

To make a Fool.

Take two quarts of cream, set it over the fire and let it boil, then take the yolks of twelve eggs and beat them very well with three or four spoonfuls of cold cream, and then strain the eggs in the *skillet* of the hot cream, stirring it all the time to keep it from burning. Then set it on the fire and let it boil a little while, but keep it still stirring for fear of burning, so then take it off and let it stand and cool, then take two or three spoonfuls of *sack* and put it in the dish, with four or five *sippets*, set the dish and sippets a-drying and when they be dry that they hang to the dish, sweeten the cream and pour it into the dish softly, because the sippets shall not rise up; this will make three dishes. When it is cold it is fit to be eaten.

To make an artichoke pie.

Take the bottom of six artichokes, being boiled very tender, put them in a dish and some vinegar over them, season them with ginger and sugar, a little mace whole, and put them in a *coffin* of paste. When you lay them in, lay some marrow and dates sliced, and a few *raisins of the sun* in the bottom, with good store of butter. When it is half baked take a gill of *sack*, being boiled first with sugar, and a peel of orange, put it in the pie and set it in the oven again until you use it.

To boil Flounders or *Jacks* after the best manner.

Take a pint of white wine, the tops of young thyme and rosemary and a little whole mace, a little whole pepper seasoned with *verjuice*, salt, and a piece of *sweet butter*, and so serve it; you may do fish in the same liquor three or four times.

To draw butter, of only use in sauces.

Take the butter and cut it into thin slices, put it into a dish, then put it upon the coals where it may melt leisurely, stir it often and when it is melted put in two or three spoonfuls of water or vinegar, which you please, then stir it and beat it until it be thick. If the colour keep white it is good, but if it look yellow and curdly in boiling it is nought, and not fit to be used to this purpose.

To make puff-paste.

Break two eggs in three pints of flour, make it with cold water, then roll it out pretty thick and square, then take so much butter as paste and divide your butter in five places, that you may lay it on at five several times, roll your paste very broad and take one part of the same butter in little pieces all over your paste, then throw a handful of flour slightly on, then fold up your paste and beat it with a rolling-pin, so roll it out again; thus do several times and then make it up.

To make an excellent Jelly.

Take three gallons of fair water, boil in it a knuckle of veal and two calves' feet slit in two with all the fat clean taken from between the claws, so let them boil to a very tender jelly keeping it clean skimmed and the edges of the pot always wiped with a clean cloth, that none of the scum may boil in them. Strain it from the meat and let it stand all night, and the next morning take away the top and the bottom, and take to a quart of this jelly half a pint of sherry *sack*, half an ounce of cinnamon and as much sugar as will season it, six whites of eggs very well beaten; mingle all these together, then boil it half an hour and let it run through your jelly bag.

Another manner
to make a fresh Cheese
presently.

Take the whites of six eggs, beat them very well and wring in the juice of a good lemon to the whites. When the cream seetheth up, put in the whites and stir it about till it be turned, and then take it off and put it into a cheese trough, and let the whey be drawn from it, then take the curd and pound it in a stone mortar with a little rose-water and sugar, and put it into an *earthen* colander, and so let it stand till you send it to the table. Then put it into a dish and put a little cream to it and so serve it.

To make a Cheese-cake
the best way.

Take two gallons of new milk, put into it two spoonfuls and a half of rennet, heat the milk little less than blood-warm, cover it close with a cloth until you see the cheese be gathered, then with a skimming dish gently take out the whey, so when you have drained the curd as clean as you can, put the curd into a sieve and let it drain very well there. Then to two quarts of curd take a quart of thick cream, a pound of sweet butter, twelve eggs, a pound and a half of currants, a pennyworth of clove, nutmeg and mace beaten, half a pound of good sugar, a quarter of a pint of rose-water, so mingle it well together and put it in puff-paste.

Another way [to make
a Cheese cake.]

Put due quantity of rennet to three gallons of milk, that it may be a tender curd, run it through a thin strainer. When it comes or gathereth, squeeze or press out the whey as well as you can possible, put it into a deep basin, put to it about a pound of sweet butter melted, sixteen eggs, casting away half the whites. Season it with beaten cinnamon, ginger, cloves, mace and nutmeg, some sugar, sufficient to sweeten it, with some salt, *eringo* and *citron* minced, a handful of grated bread or *Naples biscuit*, mix it all well together. If it be too stiff add a little sweet cream, let it not be too thin, so beat down the sides of your cakes; then make your cakes with melted butter and warm your milk with a handful of powdered sugar. Roll out your paste and *jag out* your pattern by a large round *trencher* and paper thereon, then put on the seasoned curds by spoonfuls and turn up the sides of it in six or eight corners, bake them in a quick oven but not too hot. They will ask a quarter of an hour's baking.

To broil Oysters.

Take the biggest oysters you can get, then take a little minced thyme, grated nutmeg and grated bread and a little salt, put this to the oysters, then get some of the largest bottom shells and place them on the *gridiron*, and put two or three oysters in each shell. Then put some butter to them and let them simmer on the fire till the liquor bubbles low, supplying it still with butter. When they are crisp, feed them with white wine and a little of their own liquor, with a little grated bread, nutmeg and minced thyme, but as much only as to relish it, so let it boil up again, then add some drawn butter to thicken them and dish them on a dish or plate. But if you have scallop shells it is the best way to broil them in.

To broil *Scallops.*

First boil the scallops and then take them out of the shells and wash them, then slice them and season them with nutmeg, ginger and cinnamon, and put them into the bottom of your shells again, with a little butter, white wine and vinegar and grated bread, let them be broiled on both sides. If they are sharp, they must have sugar added to them, for the fish is luscious and sweet naturally; there is therefore another proper way to broil them, with oyster liquor and gravy, with dissolved anchovies, minced onions and thyme, with the juice of a lemon in it.

To stew a dish of Trouts.

Let your frying-pan be very hot with clarified butter, then split them in two and give them a sudden brown with a forcible heat, and let a stewing dish be ready prepared with gravy, oyster liquor, a little claret wine and vinegar. Fry three of four sliced onions, and when they are brown put them to the fish, with a handful of parsley fried green, a sliced nutmeg, two or three anchovies, and let it just boil up together. Then dish up your trouts upon *sippets:* notwithstanding the best way for crispness and sight of your fish is to fry the split fish, as trout, salmon *peal* and salmon, very crisp and brown; dish it up with the inside uppermost.

To stew a Carp.

Take a living carp and knock him on the head, open him in the belly, take heed you break not the gall, pour in a little vinegar and wash out all the blood, stir it about with your hand, then keep it safe, then have a pan or *skillet* on the fire with so much white wine as will almost cover the fish; put to it an onion cut in the middle, a clove or less of garlic, a *race of ginger* shred, a nutmeg quartered, a faggot or bundle of sweet herbs, three or four anchovies. Your carp being cut out and rubbed all over with salt, when the wine (if abated with a little water will do as well) doth boil put the carp in and cover him close, and let him stew up for about a quarter of an hour, then put in the blood and vinegar with a little butter, so dish up the carp and let the spawn, milt and *rivet* be laid upon it, the liquor that boiled him, with the butter, is the best sauce, and is to be eaten as broth; garnish the dish with lemons and grated bread.

To make a *Warden*
or Pear pie.

Bake your wardens or pears in an oven, with a little water and good quantity of sugar, let your pot be covered with a piece of dough, let them not be fully baked by a quarter of an hour. When they are cold make a high *coffin* and put them in whole, adding to them some cloves, whole cinnamon, sugar, with some of the liquor they were closed in, so bake it.

To make a Quince Pie.

Cut your quinces from the core and fill your pie, lay over it sliced *orangeado* and pour into it the syrup of *barberries*, mulberries, orangeado and put on good store of sugar, with two or three sticks of cinnamon, so close it and prick it, but give it as little vent as you can; you may also bake them whole, after you have cored them with your coring iron and pared them very thin. When they are placed in your pie, fill the vacant place where your core was taken out with the syrup of orangeado, they ought to have as much sugar as their weight, but not if you have store of sweet syrup.

To make a pie with *Pippins*.

You must core and pare your pippins, and when your *coffin* is made, take a handful of sliced quinces and strew over the bottom thereof, then place in your pippins and fill the core holes with the syrup of quinces, and put into every one a piece of *orangeado*, so pour on the syrup of quinces over the apples with sugar and close it; these pies will ask good *soaking*, especially the quince pie.

To make a double Tart.

Take some *codlings* tenderly boiled and peel them, cut them in halves, fill your tart, put into a quarter of a hundred of codlings a pound and a half of sugar, a few cloves and a little cinnamon, close up the *coffin* and bake it. When it comes out of the oven take a quart of cream, six eggs, a *quartern* of sugar and a *sliced nutmeg*, beat all these well together, pour them into the tart, then set your tart in the oven for half a quarter of an hour. When it comes out cut off the *ley* and having a lid cut in flowers ready, lay it on and garnish it with preserves of damsons, raspberries, apricots and cherries, and place a preserved quince in the middle and strew it with sugar biscuits.

How to make an Almond Tart.

Raise an excellent good paste with six corners, an inch deep, take some blanched almonds very finely beaten with rose-water. Take a pound of sugar to a pound of almonds, some grated nutmeg, a little cream, with strained spinach as much as will colour the almonds green, so bake it with a gentle heat in an oven, not shutting the lid, draw it, and stick it with candied orange and citron and red and white *muscadine*.

To make white Quince Cakes.

First clarify the sugar with the white of an egg, but put not so much water to it as you do for marmalade; before you clarify it, keep out almost a quarter of the sugar, let your quinces be scalded and let them be chopped in small pieces before you put it into the syrup, then make it boil as fast as you can, and when you have skimmed it and you think it be half boiled, then *jamire* it, and let the other part of your sugar be ready candied to a hard candy, and so put them together, letting it boil but a very little after the candy is put to it, then put in a little *musk*, and so lay it out before it be cold.

To make red Quince Cakes.

Bake them in an oven with some of their own juice, their own cores being cut or bruised and put to them, then weigh some of this juice with some of the quince, being cut into small pieces, taking their weight in sugar, and with the quince, some pretty quantity of juice of *barberries*, being baked or stewed in a pot; when you have taken their weight in sugar you must put the weighed quince, and above three quarters of the sugar together, and put to it some little quantity of water as you shall see cause, but make not the syrup too thin; and when you have put all this together, cover it and set it to the fire, keep it covered and skim it as much as you can; when it is half boiled, then simmer it; let the other part of sugar have no more water put to it than will wet the sugar and so let it be boiled to a very hard candy, and when you think they be boiled enough then lay them out before they be cold.

To make clear cakes of Quince.

You must prepare the quinces and *barberries* as before, and then take the clearest syrup and let it stand on the coals two or three hours. Then take the weight of it in sugar and put near half the sugar to the juice and so let them boil a little on the fire and then candy the rest of the sugar very hard, and so put them together, stirring it while it is almost cold, and so put it into glasses.

To preserve Quinces white.

Take to every pound of quince a pound and a quarter of sugar, clarify this sugar with the white of an egg, core your quinces but not too much, and then put this sugar, and water, and quince, being raw, together, and so make them boil so fast as you can see no quince, but forget not to turn them and take off what skim you can, keep them boiling thus fast till you think they be enough.

*A*nd so I have run through the whole and more usual fare of her private table, observing no method therein because I had them in this form from a near servant of hers. As for Fish and Flesh days, there was no observation of them, all days being alike to the caterer and purveyor and those that eat at her tables, as was hinted before. ❡ But this habit of diet not proving effectual to the prolongation of Oliver's life, by and with which this Court subsisted, and was the only ligament of that riff raff society, a *voider* was the next service; for though there were some faint and slight shows of house-

Voider: a receptacle into which dirty dishes, utensils, fragments of broken food were placed when clearing the table.

keeping, which the standing Court Officers maintained with their credit (and injury of several persons who trusted upon the greatness of the deceased usurper) to keep their places warm and themselves in action; yet Mrs. Cromwell wifely and timely withdrew her stake and suffered her son "Ricardo" to run the risk of the old and new debt upon his own score. ⁋ And upon his account merely was that costly solemnity of Oliver's funerals advised, on purpose to bankrupt him; the pomp bestowed on the dead proving the ruin and disgrace of the living, so that all things went backward with him with double the pace they flowed upon his father, and in the same manner; for whereas his father was wont to call in the Guards to eat the relics of his victuals, now they rushed in and perforce took the meat off his table, with demand of their pay and arrears; and this with so much insolence that Mrs. Cromwell, the afflicted mother of this Unfortunatus, could not forbear in anger to tell her son Fleetwood, "That he had brought his hogs to a fair market". Nor is all that droll which is mentioned of her in a play, called **"The Rump, or Mirror of the Times"**.[50]

FINIS

GLOSSARY

Ambergris:	a grey substance like dried putty, produced from a secretion of the sperm whale. It has a perfume like the blending of new-mown hay with the scent of violets.
Aviled:	degraded.
Barberries:	oblong, red, sharply acid berries, the fruit of the shrub "Berberis vulgaris". As well as being used in the kitchen, barberries were also used medicinally for ailments of the gall bladder, liver and kidneys. It is interesting to note that Oliver Cromwell suffered with kidney stones and gravel in the kidneys.
Beaten ginger:	root ginger, well bruised. Many recipes contain "beaten" spices. The spice was no doubt pounded with a pestle and mortar.
Beer-vinegar:	malt vinegar.
Blue currants:	apparently the usual dry currants, which are, of course, not really currants but small dried black grapes.
Borage:	"Borago officinalis" – mostly used today in summer wine cups and drinks. Has a strong onion-like smell and a spicy cucumber-like taste. Medicinally, it is good for the kidneys as it has a mildly diuretic effect.
Brewis:	bread soaked in gravy.
Broach:	a tapering, pointed instrument; a spit for roasting meat.
Broom buds:	"Sarothamnus scoparius" – the common yellow broom of the hedgerows in limefree soil. Now regarded as unreliable and only used under medical supervision.
Bugloss:	"Echium vulgare" – coarse, hairy leaves and blue flowers. The young shoots may be treated and eaten like spinach.
Bustard:	the Great Bustard, sometimes also called the "Fen Bustard". A large bird somewhat resembling a turkey, once common in East Anglia but now extinct.

Capers:	the pickled flower buds of a bramble-type Mediterranean shrub. In this country pickled nasturtium seeds are often used as a substitute.
Cap-paper:	a kind of coarse paper, wrapping paper.
Carbonadoed:	meat scored with a knife before cooking.
Cardoon or Cardone:	"Cynara cardunculus" – a plant closely related to the artichoke, grown for its celery-like stalks. Cultivated in Europe and introduced into England about 1656.
Case:	to skin.
Caudle:	a warm drink consisting of thin gruel mixed with wine or ale, sweetened and spiced.
Caul:	the net-like, fatty membrane which encloses the intestines of the animal. Sometimes used today to wrap meat for barbecue cooking.
Chafing-dish:	a vessel to hold burning charcoal or other fuel, for warming food at the table.
China or China-root:	a plant (Smilax china) closely akin to Sarsaparilla, the powdered root of which is still used as a tonic and blood purifier.
Citron:	a Mediterranean fruit "Citrus medica", somewhat resembling a lemon. The name is now restricted to a pale yellow oval fruit, larger and less acid than a lemon; but in the 17th century "citron" would have included both lemon and lime.
Cock:	woodcock.
Codlings:	a variety of apple.
Cods:	pods.
Coffin:	a pie crust; a mould of paste for a pie. The word has been known in this sense since 1420.
Colewort:	any plant of the cabbage family.
Collop:	a small piece or slice of boneless meat
Drawn:	difficult to determine whether this means "infused" or "drawn from the oven" in several cases.
Drive forth: Drive out:	roll out (pastry).
Earthen colander:	earthenware (coarse country pottery) i.e. a metal colander should not be used.

Elder vinegar:	vinegar in which dried elder flowers have been steeped. According to Gerard's *Herball* (1597) "being used with meat it stirreth up an appetite".
Eringo:	also spelt eryngo; the candied root of sea-holly, "Eryngium". A member of the carrot family, with a similar taste.
Farcing:	forcemeat stuffing.
Fearce:	untraceable except as an old spelling of "fierce". The sense seems to indicate that the birds should be seared (by a "fierce" heat?) to remove the feathers.
Figures:	beans and turnips cut into various decorative shapes.
Flayed:	skinned – original spells it "flead".
Fleck of pork:	also spelt "flick"; the inside fat of the pig, which is melted down for lard, or the fat of pork next to the skin.
Fried green (marrow):	an untraceable phrase. Could mean "fresh" marrow (from marrow bones). Bones are said to be "green" if healthy and full of marrow.
Gold:	see notes.
Grain:	the smallest English measure, about $\frac{1}{7000}$ part of a pound weight. Originally the weight of one grain of wheat.
Gridiron:	a frame of iron bars for broiling over a fire.
Groat:	a silver coin, value 4d (about 1½p) about the size of a present day 1p.
Gross:	coarse.
Hackney turnips:	Hackney was a market gardening area on the outskirts of London in the 17th century.
Harts-horn:	the buckthorn (Rhamnus catharticus), the berries of which are a powerful laxative.
Interlarded:	strips of fat bacon, etc. inserted into lean meat before cooking.
Jacks:	small, or young, pike; sometimes used as a general name for a pike.
Jag Out:	to cut out a rough paper shape for pastry etc. by cutting it round a plate.
Jamire:	untraceable word but sense implies "test for setting".
Lambstones:	the testicles of a lamb.
Larding pin:	a pointed instrument with which meat is pierced and pieces of fat bacon inserted for cooking.
Lear:	a thickened sauce.

Ley:	untraceable in this context. The sense seems to indicate "take off the lid that was baked on the pie". Elisabeth Ayrton in *The Cookery of England* writes "In earlier times a pie was often partly cooked with a false lid made of flour and watercrust, which was broken away and replaced by the rich pastry lid, just as we replace foil with pastry today".
Lines:	phrase untraceable but not crucial to the recipe.
Manchet:	the finest kind of wheaten bread.
Maw:	the stomach of an animal.
Muscadine:	a variety of grape or a variety of pear, with the flavour or smell of musk. Wine made from same.
Muscadoes:	probably a mis-spelling of "muscardine" (see above).
Musk:	gland from musk deer used mainly in perfume and occasionally in confectionery.
Naples biscuit:	not known exactly, obviously a cake or biscuit peculiar to Naples or Italy. The *Oxford English Dictionary* mentions "cakes or loaves cut longwise in the shape of Naples Biscuit".
Neat's tongue:	a "neat" is an ox, bullock, cow or heifer.
Orangeado:	candied orange peel, variously spelt "oringado" and "orangado" in original.
Peal:	a grilse i.e. a young salmon or sea-trout.
Peck:	a measure used for both liquids and dry goods equal to 2 gallons or ¼ of a bushel (approx. 9 litres).
Peepers:	young chickens or pigeons.
Pennyroyal:	a herb, the smallest of the mints (Mentha pulegium).
Pickle cucumbers:	gherkins. Could be used either fresh or pickled.
Pierce the gravy:	meaning uncertain but probably "pour off".
Pipkin:	a small pot or pan; may be either earthenware or metal.
Pippins:	a general term for many varieties of apple.
Pistaches:	pistachio nuts.
Pottle:	a measure equal to 2 quarts or half a gallon (a little over 2 litres).

Powdered:	salted or pickled meat.
Prick them up:	skewer them together.
Punnado:	meaning uncertain, may be derived from Portuguese word "punhado" – a handful.
Qualm:	to boil.
Quartern:	a quarter of various weight and measures.
Race of cinnamon:	This is an error as "race" is a root-stock and the term is generally applied to ginger. Cinnamon is the bark of a tree, so it can only mean here "stick cinnamon", or "quill cinnamon".
Race of ginger:	a root-stock of ginger, now usually known as "root ginger".
Raisins of the Sun:	sun dried grapes.
Red cock:	red grouse, a reddish coloured game-bird.
Rivet:	the liver of a fish, spelt "revet" in original.
Rozin:	rosin or resin – a gum obtained from plants and herbs or distilled from turpentine.
Sack:	strong white wine, probably imported from Spain or the Canaries.
Samphire:	"Crithmum maritimum" – a wild plant found growing on the sea shore, mainly along the coasts of East Anglia. The aromatic fleshy leaves are salted, boiled and pickled in spiced vinegar.
Scallops:	a shell-fish, on whose fan-shaped shell the "Shell" oil trademark is based. The white meat of the muscle is the part usually eaten today, but the prominent orange roe or "coral" is sometimes included.
Scotch:	score, cut.
Searsed, Searst:	sieved or strained.
Send it smoking up:	to serve it very hot.
Sippets:	small pieces of toasted or fried bread.
Skillet:	a metal cooking utensil which has been described as "a frying-pan on legs". The name may also be used for any saucepan or stewpan.
Skirrets:	a species of water parsnip, formerly much cultivated in Europe for its tubers which seem to have resembled dahlia tubers or potatoes in appearance.
Sliced nutmeg:	it would seem almost impossible to slice a nutmeg! This must refer to "ground nutmeg".

Small beer:	weak beer, sometimes of poor or inferior quality.
Soak, soaking:	to bake thoroughly.
Sops:	bread dipped or soaked in some liquid.
Sorrel:	a herb of the dock family, with an acid, sour taste.
Strained almonds:	crushed or pressed almonds. The modern equivalent would be ground almonds.
Sugar Peas:	"Mangetout" or edible-podded peas.
Sweet butter:	unsalted butter.
Sweet milk:	fresh milk, not sour milk.
Trencher:	a plate; sometimes a flat piece of wood on which meat was served and cut up.
Tunnel:	a funnel.
Verjuice:	the acid juice of green or unripe grapes, crab-apples or other sour fruit.
Vial:	another word for "phial", a small glass bottle.
Walm:	to boil.
Warden pears:	an old variety of pear, supposed to have been grown originally by the monks of Warden Abbey, Bedfordshire.
While:	until.
White:	uncertain – could be white sugar.
Whole cinnamon:	stick cinnamon or "quill cinnamon".
Winter-savory:	a herb (Satureia montana) with a strong, aromatic, peppery taste; good for gastric or digestive complaints. Leaves are used in salami.

NOTES

1. Henry CROMWELL – 4th son of Oliver Cromwell, born at Huntingdon 1628. Entered the Parliamentary army and was a Colonel by 1650. Took part in the Irish campaign and became major-general of the forces in Ireland and member of the Irish Council, 1654. Lord Deputy of Ireland, 1657. Urged his father to refuse the title of King. Governor-general of Ireland, 1658. Returned to England on orders of new government, 1659, and retired to Cambridgeshire. Died aged 47 on 23 March, 1673–4, and is buried in Wicken Church.

2. Charles FLEETWOOD – Major-General in Cromwell's army and his intimate friend. 3rd son of Sir Miles Fleetwood of Aldwinkle, Northants. Married, 1652 (2nd wife) Cromwell's daughter Bridget, widow of Henry Ireton.

Richard CROMWELL – 3rd son of Oliver Cromwell, born 1626. Succeeded his father as Lord Protector in 1658, but fled to Europe in early 1660, where he lived until 1680. Returning to England, he lived in retirement at Cheshunt until his death in 1712.

John DESBOROUGH – 2nd son of James Desborough of Eltisley, Cambs. Married (1636) Jane Cromwell, sister of the Lord Protector. Became a Major-General in the Parliamentary army but was always more concerned with his own interests than anything else. He would have liked to introduce a military despotism with himself in high authority, but it is said he lacked all the qualities of a statesman.

3. Restitution – the Restoration of the monarchy. Richard Cromwell retired from government in 1659, and King Charles II returned from exile in May 1660.

4. "One day it will delight us to remember even this".

5. Roman emperor A.D. 37–41, notorious for excessive and motiveless cruelty and licentiousness.

6. This quotation is from PERSIUS, Satire I, line 43. Its literal meaning refers to "herring" or "mackerel" ("schombros") and "spice" ("thus", usually spelt "tus", meaning "incense" or "spices"). Persius uses the phrase in a discussion on the fate of some writers works, i.e. they may be used as waste paper for wrapping up groceries. A free modern translation here might say "may the records of his crimes be used for wrapping up fish and chips".

7. Lambert SIMNEL (c. 1475–1525) – a poor boy who was taken up by conspirators into a plot to overthrow King Henry VII. He was persuaded to impersonate Edward, Earl of Warwick, and claim the crown, with disastrous results for all concerned. Lambert Simnel himself was eventually pardoned by Henry VII and employed as a turnspit in the royal kitchen.

8. Literally, a "something": an indescribable mixture. A name given to small dishes, usually sweet, which contained an extraordinary mixture of ingredients. They were popular in the 16th and 17th centuries and often known in England as "Kickshaws".

9. A more modern translation might read "biting and gnawing cares".

10. "The man over whose accursed head the drawn sword hangs poised – for him the Sicilian feast provides no sweet savour".

11. Elizabeth BOWCHER – Mrs. Cromwell's maiden name, usually spelt BOURCHIER. For details of her life, see Note 14.

12. A nickname given to Mrs. Cromwell by contemporary satirists. By the mid-17th century the name "Joan" was used as an insult. For details of Mrs. Cromwell's life, see Note 14.

13. This extract is taken from PERSIUS, Satire I, Line 58. According to the standard texts (Oxford and Loeb editions) the word "pinxit" should read "pinsit". The phrase may then be translated as "Happy is the man whom no stork can peck from behind", i.e., who cannot be ridiculed behind his back.

14. Elizabeth CROMWELL – daughter of a well-to-do London fur-dealer and leather-dresser, Sir James Bourchier. She and Oliver Cromwell were married in August 1620, at St. Giles Church, Cripplegate, in the City of London. They lived at Huntingdon, St. Ives and Ely before Oliver became Lord Protector, and had 8 children, 4 boys and 4 girls. After Oliver's death in 1658, Mrs. Cromwell made her home with her widowed son-in-law, John Claypole, at Northborough Castle, near Peterborough. She died in 1665 and is buried in Northborough Church.

15. "God will provide".

16. A battle during the Civil War, fought near York on July 2, 1644, between the Royalist army under Prince Rupert and the Parliamentarians. The latter were victorious but there were heavy losses on both sides.

17. Bel is the name of the Assyrio-Babylonian gods En-lil and Marduk. It has the same meaning as Baal. The story of Bel and the Dragon, in which we are told how Daniel convinced the King that Bel was not an actual living deity but only an image, was formerly part of the book of Daniel, but is now relegated to the Apocrypha.

18. Probably Francisco de GUZMAN, Spanish poet, author of "Triumphos Morales", 1565.

19. A mock autobiography, first published anonymously in Spain in 1554. It is really a short 'picaresque' novel which is a social satire on various aspects of contemporary Spain. Religious and philosophical morals may also be drawn from it, especially the contention that we are all hypocrites, deceiving ourselves as much as we deceive others. The work was translated into several languages and has gone through numerous editions right up to the present day.

20. Barten HOLYDAY – 17th century author and translator of classical poetry (Horace, Juvenal and Persius).

21. A more modern translation: "You ask strength for your nerves and a body that is sound [even] in old age. Well then, so be it, but your huge dishes and your fat sausages forbid the gods on high to grant this, and they hinder Jupiter".

22. Translated into Roman Alphabet this quotation reads:– "SOPHROSYNEN LEGESTHAI HOS SOZOSAN TEN PHRONESIN, KAI AULEN PSYCHEN EINAI SOPHO-TATEN" and may be translated more or less literally as "it is called moderation as it preserves sense; and the soul is the dwelling-place of wisdom". EPICTETUS was a Stoic philosopher who was teaching between c. A.D.55 and c. A.D. 135.

23. A more modern translation: "In our feasting, we should keep separate two guests, Body and Spirit. For then, what is put into the body will suddenly pass away, but what is put into the soul (or mind) is to be retained there for ever".

24. "In truth your suppers are delightful, not only at the time, but on the following day, as well".

25. Elizabeth CLAYPOLE (née CROMWELL) – Oliver's second daughter and favourite child – "Bettie". Born at Huntingdon, 1629, she married John Claypole of North-borough Castle, at Ely in 1646. She died, probably of cancer, at the age of 29. Oliver survived her by barely a month and is said never to have recovered from her death. She was buried in Westminster Abbey and her tomb was allowed to remain there after the Restoration.

26. John CLAYPOLE – a country gentleman, of North-borough Castle, near Peterborough. Although not essentially a military man, he supported the Parliamentary cause and took part in various Civil War engagements. Appointed Cromwell's Master of the Horse, 1653. Married Cromwell's second daughter "Bettie", at Ely, in January 1646. She died in 1658. After Oliver's death and the family's disgrace, John Claypole gave his mother-in-law, Elizabeth (the subject of this book) a home with him at Northborough until her own death in 1665. She is buried there. He died in poverty in London in 1688, having already sold his Northborough estate to Lord Fitzwilliam.

27. A house in the village of Basing, Hampshire, built by the first Marquess of Winchester (d. 1572), famous for its stout resistance, under the fifth Marquess, to the Parliamentarian forces for two years. The defenders finally yielded to Cromwell himself (1645), when architect Inigo Jones was one of the prisoners taken. Little now remains except the 16th century gatehouse and dovecote.

28. "No one approached so soberly the task of overthrowing the state".

29. An ultra-Republican extremist party, leader John Lilburne. Formed about 1647, they considered the existing Republic too aristocratic and little better than the monarchy. They acquired a strong following in the Army, where there was already discontent over arrears of pay and service conditions. Criticisms of the regime mounted, some prominent Levellers were arrested and mutiny broke out in the Army. This was quickly put down and the Levellers' movement came to an end. Cromwell was accused by critics of deceit and hypocrisy.

30. One of the great historical fairs which dealt in cloth, livestock etc. accompanied by a variety of amusements and entertainments. It opened annually on St. Bartholomew's Day (Aug. 24) and was last held in 1855. The Caledonian Market, which opened in that year, is a relic of the Fair. "Bartholomew Fair" was a centre for London life, and the Puritans failed to suppress it. Ben Jonson's 'comedy of manners' "Bartholomew Fair" was first presented in 1614.

31. A fable by La Fontaine which appears in a modern translation by Edward Marsh as "Cat into Lady". The point made by the fable is that the characteristics we are born with rule us till we die.

32. Madam PRIDE – wife of Thomas PRIDE (see note 41).

Lady HEWSON – wife of John Hewson, soldier and officer in the Parliamentary army, M.P. and member of Cromwell's House of Lords. He was one of the King's judges and signed the death-warrant, 1649. Becoming extremely unpopular, he fled the country at the Restoration and died abroad.

Lady BERKSTEAD or BARKSTEAD – wife of Sir John Barkstead, an officer in the Parlimentary army who was one of King Charles' judges in 1648. Knighted in 1656 and appointed Steward of Cromwell's household. Fled to the Continent at the Restoration (1660) but was arrested in Holland, 1661, brought to England and executed 1662. Notorious for his cruelty.

Lady GOFF (otherwise spelt GOFFE or GOUGH) – wife of Colonel William Goffe, officer in the Parliamentary army. One of the King's judges, 1648; Major-General for Berkshire, Sussex and Hampshire, 1655; member of Cromwell's House of Lords. At the Restoration fled with Edward Whalley (his father-in-law) to Massachusetts; lived concealed for three years; traditionally supposed to have repelled an attack of Indians at Hadley, Massachusetts, 1675; died about 1679 and is buried at Hadley. His wife and family remained in England.

Lady WHALLEY – wife of Edward Whalley, a soldier in Cromwell's army rising to rank of Major General. He sat as a judge and signed Charles I's death-warrant. Their daughter Frances married Major-General William Goffe (q.v.).

33. The term applied contemptuously to the remnant of the "Long Parliament" (1640–1660) which was left after 'Pride's Purge' (see Note 41). It abolished the House of Lords and the monarchy and declared England a Commonwealth.

34. A more modern translation: "It requires the same power of thought to organize a battle and a feast – the battle line so that it may seem terrifying to the enemy, the feast to be pleasing to friends".

35. Thomas FAIRFAX (1612–1671) – 3rd Baron Fairfax of Cameron. Professional soldier; became a General in the Parliamentary Army 1642 and distinguished himself in many Civil War campaigns. Reorganised the Army into what was known as the "New Model Army". One of the King's judges, 1649, endeavouring to prevent his execution. Headed the commission sent to Charles II at the Hague, 1660; retired to Yorkshire, died 1671. Buried in Bilbrough Church, near York.

36. May refer to Kate, Lady d'Aubigny, widow of Lord George d'Aubigny who was imprisoned for her part in a Royalist plot to seize the Tower and arrest the Parliamentary Leaders. Died in exile at The Hague, 1650.

37. Almost up to the present century the carving of meat was considered an important skill. In the 14th and 15th century the carver's position was high in the household hierarchy; the royal carvers were knights who ranked immediately after the nobles. In noble households the Carver was often a Squire. Somewhat later – probably near Mrs. Cromwell's time – carving schools using wooden demonstration models were started in Italy, and it is to these that the following quotation refers.

38. This extract is from JUVENAL Satire XV, lines 138–141. The standard translation ("Loeb" edition, 1918) reads: ". . . (in whose school) is cut up, with blunt knives, a magnificent feast of hares and sow's paunches, of boars and antelopes, of Scythian fowls and tall flamingoes and Gaetulian gazelles, until the whole Subura rings with the clatter of the elm-wood banquet".
"The Subura" was a slum quarter of Rome.
"Scythian fowls" are believed to have been pheasants.

39. Colonel Philip JONES (1618?–1674) – Welsh parliamentarian, governor of Swansea and one of Cromwell's peers. Controller of the Household to Oliver and Richard Cromwell. He acquired a large fortune and was charged with corruption by the military party and extreme republicans. Made his peace with the King and was Sheriff of Glamorgan 1671.

40. Miles SYNDERCOMBE (otherwise spelt SINDERCOMBE) – a Royalist activist who attempted to assassinate Oliver Cromwell. He was arrested and committed suicide in the Tower in February 1657.

41. Thomas PRIDE – entered Cromwell's army as a Captain and commanded Harley's regiment at Naseby in 1645. In 1648, in order to frustrate the intended agreement with Charles I, he prevented about 130 members from entering the House of Commons ("Pride's Purge"). Pride opposed Cromwell's appointment as King but accepted a seat in his upper house. He became rich enough to buy Nonesuch Park and House in Surrey and in 1655–6 was High Sheriff of the county. Died and was buried at Nonesuch, 1658.

42. Duc de CREQUI (1623–1687) – Charles III of the "House of Crequi", a French noble family. Became Duc de Crequi in 1653, fought at Rocroi and Nordlingen, and became French ambassador at Rome in 1662. It is recorded that while there he quarrelled with the Papal Guard. Later became Governor of Paris (1676) and Ambassador to Britain (1677).

43. Probably Michele Lorenzo MANCINI, Italian nobleman, who was introduced to the French court following his marriage (1656) to Girolama MAZARINI, the sister of Cardinal Mazarini ("Jules Mazarin") the great French statesman. They had many descendents, most of whom were involved in French politics.

44. Oysters are used generously in several recipes. It should be remembered that until about 1850 oysters were so plentiful and cheap that they were the common food of even the poorest people. It is not known how much Mrs. Cromwell would have paid for her oysters; but, in 1700, 200 cost 4/- (20p).

45. Apart from being valued in the usual ways, gold was believed to have other mysterious properties. The old Alchemists believed that the Philosopher's Stone, if it could be found, would be gold of enormously exalted purity, and would be a universal remedy for human ills and diseases. Gold salts are in fact still used in medical treatment. In short, boiling in the "3 or 4 pieces of Gold" would be considered to be "good for you".

46. Frances CROMWELL – Oliver's youngest daughter, born at Ely in 1638. She married, first, Robert Rich, grandson of Lord Warwick, but was widowed after only 3 months. Later she married again, this time to Sir John Russell of Chippenham. They had many descendants. Frances lived until 1721 and is buried in St. Nicholas Church, Chiswick, with her sister Mary (Lady Fauconberg).

47. Meaning is uncertain as the word "carior" does not appear in this form in any likely source. The word CARRIER, however, has been used since at least Shakespeare's time, for a "bearer of information". It seems to have been used in a derogatory sense and there may perhaps be some connection – "to steal a march on the carrier", by publishing a supposed tit-bit of gossip before it was spread abroad by other means.

48. A highly flavoured dish, or a piquant flavour; also an unpleasant taste or smell.

49. Literally, a horse-soldier wearing a cuirass, which was a piece of armour for the body. The word was introduced in the 17th century and was applied to the heavy cavalry in the Civil wars. Obviously used here figuratively.

50. A play (1661) by John Tatham, a minor dramatist of whose personal history little is known. He was a fervent Cavalier who hated all Puritans.